An Apology for the Conduct of the Gordons; Containing the whole of their Correspondence, Conversation, &c. With MRS. Lee. To Which is Annexed, An accurate Account of their Trial at Oxford.

Loudoun Harcourt Gordon

An Apology for the Conduct of the Gordons; Containing the whole of their Correspondence, Conversation,&c. With MRS. Lee. To Which is Annexed, An accurate Account of their Trail at oxford.

Apology for the conduct of Lockhart Gordon & L.H.
Loudoun Harcourt Gordon
NYB01278
Monograph
New York City Bar
London: Printed for John Ginger, 169, Piccadilly; and Thomas Hurst, Paternoster-row. 1804.

The Making of Modern Law collection of legal archives constitutes a genuine revolution in historical legal research because it opens up a wealth of rare and previously inaccessible sources in legal, constitutional, administrative, political, cultural, intellectual, and social history. This unique collection consists of three extensive archives that provide insight into more than 300 years of American and British history. These collections include:

Legal Treatises, 1800-1926: over 20,000 legal treatises provide a comprehensive collection in legal history, business and economics, politics and government.

Trials, 1600-1926: nearly 10,000 titles reveal the drama of famous, infamous, and obscure courtroom cases in America and the British Empire across three centuries.

Primary Sources, 1620-1926: includes reports, statutes and regulations in American history, including early state codes, municipal ordinances, constitutional conventions and compilations, and law dictionaries.

These archives provide a unique research tool for tracking the development of our modern legal system and how it has affected our culture, government, business – nearly every aspect of our everyday life. For the first time, these high-quality digital scans of original works are available via print-on-demand, making them readily accessible to libraries, students, independent scholars, and readers of all ages.

The BiblioLife Network

This project was made possible in part by the BiblioLife Network (BLN), a project aimed at addressing some of the huge challenges facing book preservationists around the world. The BLN includes libraries, library networks, archives, subject matter experts, online communities and library service providers. We believe every book ever published should be available as a high-quality print reproduction; printed on-demand anywhere in the world. This insures the ongoing accessibility of the content and helps generate sustainable revenue for the libraries and organizations that work to preserve these important materials.

The following book is in the "public domain" and represents an authentic reproduction of the text as printed by the original publisher. While we have attempted to accurately maintain the integrity of the original work, there are sometimes problems with the original work or the micro-film from which the books were digitized. This can result in minor errors in reproduction. Possible imperfections include missing and blurred pages, poor pictures, markings and other reproduction issues beyond our control. Because this work is culturally important, we have made it available as part of our commitment to protecting, preserving, and promoting the world's literature.

GUIDE TO FOLD-OUTS MAPS and OVERSIZED IMAGES

The book you are reading was digitized from microfilm captured over the past thirty to forty years. Years after the creation of the original microfilm, the book was converted to digital files and made available in an online database.

In an online database, page images do not need to conform to the size restrictions found in a printed book. When converting these images back into a printed bound book, the page sizes are standardized in ways that maintain the detail of the original. For large images, such as fold-out maps, the original page image is split into two or more pages

Guidelines used to determine how to split the page image follows:

• Some images are split vertically; large images require vertical and horizontal splits.
• For horizontal splits, the content is split left to right.
• For vertical splits, the content is split from top to bottom.
• For both vertical and horizontal splits, the image is processed from top left to bottom right.

3.

AN
APOLOGY

FOR THE

CONDUCT OF THE GORDONS;

CONTAINING THE WHOLE OF THEIR

CORRESPONDENCE, CONVERSATION, &c

WITH

MRS. LEE:

~~~~~~

TO WHICH IS ANNEXED,
AN ACCURATE ACCOUNT
OF THEIR
EXAMINATION AT BOW STREET,
AND THEIR
TRIAL AT OXFORD.

BY

LOUDOUN HARCOURT GORDON, Esq.

NON JOVI DATUR SAPERE ET AMARE

LONDON
PRINTED FOR JOHN GINGER, 169, PICCADILLY;
AND
THOMAS HURST, PATERNOSTER-ROW

1804.

INTRODUCTION.

SOME apology is certainly due to the Public for this appeal to them, which would not have been made, had not my own and my brother's Trial been put an end to previously to our entering upon our Defence; in the course of which, I have no hesitation in saying, that we should have been enabled to prove that the appearance of force, which was made use of to conceal Mrs. Lee's wishes and intentions from her servants, was the consequence of a previous arrangement between Mrs. Lee and myself for her elopement; and had not the evidence given upon my own and my brother's Trial been misrepresented in a variety of publications.

Unacquainted with the rules of composition, and uninstructed in the art of making the " worse appear the better reason," I humbly submit to an enlightened and liberal Public, an accurate statement of the whole of my brother's and my own conduct towards Mrs. Lee, from the renewal of our acquaintance with her, in December last; together with an impartial account of our Trial, which has been copied from notes taken by my brother Lockhart in Court.

It is not my intention to attempt a vindication of my own or my brother's conduct, but merely to assert, and I trust that I shall be enabled to prove to the Public, that we have been the dupes of an artful and treacherous woman; who, in her turn, has been compelled to serve the interested and mercenary purposes of others.

Mrs. Lee (then Miss Dashwood) resided at my mother's house in Kensington Square, during the greater part of the years 1789 and 1790, and was the only young person at that time under Mrs. Gordon's protection. Lockhart and myself were then at different schools, and during the holydays we lived upon terms of the greatest familiarity with Mrs. Lee. No intercourse took place between Miss Dashwood and Mrs Gordon after she left my mother, owing probably to Miss Dashwood's living in the house with her mother.

At the age of fourteen I was admitted a Cadet at the Royal Military Academy, at Woolwich, and obtained a Commission in the Artillery when sixteen years old In 1797 I went to Martinique, in February, 1798, I was compelled to return to Europe by ill health: in the the month of June following, I returned to the West Indies, and remained there until July, 1803, when, having been superseded in the Army for having taken the benefit of an Act for the further relief of insolvent debtors, I returned to England and arrived at Liverpool on the 19th of October last, soon after which I went to London, and on my brother's return to Town, lodged with him for some time in the house where he had lived more than two years. The usual enquiries after former acquaintance, induced me to ask Lockhart if he knew what was become of Miss Dashwood. Lockhart said that he believed she had married, was separated, and lived at Woodford. A bilious complaint occasioned my calling upon Mr. Blackett, on the 2nd of December, 1803, who had for many years attended my mother's family as her Apothecary. Amongst others of my former acquaintance I asked Mr. Blackett if he knew any thing of Miss Dashwood. Mr. Blackett told me that she was now Mrs. Lee, and lived at Woodford, but that she either had taken a house or was about to take one in Bolton Row, Piccadilly. Mr. Blackett has since said, that he had a private reason for not informing me where Mrs. Lee lived. When Mr. Blackett informed Mrs. Lee that I had made enquiries after her, she desired Mr. Blackett " to let Loudoun know that she should be happy to see him." Mr. Blackett mentioned that circumstance to me during my confinement in the new Prison, Clerkenwell. I accidentally heard, a few days after my having seen Mr. Blackett, where Mrs. Lee lived, and called upon her for the first time, on the evening of the 14th of

December. The impression which the charms of Miss Dashwood had made upon my mind, in childhood, was not effaced; separated from her by many hundred leagues, amidst the terrors of a vertical sun, I have frequently contemplated with melancholy pleasure upon her beauty and talents, which even during infancy had created a lasting passion in my breast. The warm reception which I received from Mrs. Lee, rekindled the latent flame; my own inclination, united to the artful pro-vocations made use of by Mrs. Lee to effect her wishes, soon deprived me of all power of resistance or reflection. I was insensibly ensnared, and unconscious of the criminality of my conduct, I submitted to the importunity with which Mrs. Lee unceasingly endeavoured to persuade me to use my influence to induce Lockhart to visit her. Unhappily my endeavours were but too successful. What I have suffered or may do, for myself it is nothing, but I shall for ever deplore the fate of an affectionate brother, who has been condemned unheard.

During my second visit to Mrs. Lee, on the 16th of December, she told me that she was then writing a letter to excuse her going to Bath, which she had intended to do.

What could induce Mrs Lee to alter her intention of going to Bath so suddenly? Was it the fear of losing an Hebrew lesson by Mr Friend, the once well-known ci-devant Fellow of Jesus College, Cambridge, in a morning? Or was it to avoid the disappointment which Mrs. Lee would feel at not having an evening tete-a-tete with Sir William Beachey? Whatever was the whim of the moment, Mrs. Lee remained in London, and appointed the 24th of December for our next interview. On that day Mrs. Lee gave me the paper containing what she then was pleased to tell me was her dream, she has since confessed it was a fiction. For what?—I leave the unprejudiced reader to define the motive which induced a married woman, who was in the most delicate of all situations in which a married woman can possibly be placed, to trump up a parcel of nonsensical words, which will readily bear a most indecent interpretation, and to communicate such ribaldry to a very young man, who she well knew had passed the latter part of his life in the Army. The erasure of her name from the bottom of the fictitious Dream was the first proof of the cautious turpitude, with which Mrs Lee has invariably acted towards me Most unhappily for Mrs. Lee, for my brother, for myself, for every one who is so unfortunate as to be most distantly connected with us, I shewed the Dream to Lockhart, with Mrs. Lee's previous consent He immediately told me that it would bear a religious interpretation, and gave me the outline of that exposition which I afterwards transmitted to Mrs. Lee, and which is faithfully transcribed from the original manuscript, for the inspection of the public, in the following pages.

The voice of scandal which has been so loud against my brother and myself, will, I trust, be silenced by the religious and moral tendency of what the Public have been induced to believe was written in the most indecent language, to serve the most infamous purposes. Far be it from me to treat the hallowed subject of Christianity with unbecoming levity. The only motive which could induce Lockhart to lend his assistance, must have been a sincere desire to point out to Mrs. Lee, in the only way which was likely to be effectual, the weakness and wickedness of scepticism. I trust that what was written with so good an intention will not be wholly useless.

Mrs. Lee lived for some years in a Convent in France, and early imbibed the dogmas of that false philosophy which has since given rise to all the crimes and madness of the dreadful Revolution, which has so long devastated that unhappy country. Upon Mrs. Lee's return to England, she was placed under the protection of my mother, it was to have been hoped that she would have derived benefit from the virtuous precepts and exemplary conduct of a learned, a pious, and an enlightened christian.

On Friday, the 30th of December, Lockhart called with me upon Mrs. Lee, about one o'clock, in consequence of her repeated and pressing request that he would do so. Her insinuating conduct cannot be more forcibly exemplified than by a perusal of the conversation which took place on that day   The melancholy detail which she gave of her situation must have excited the commiseration of the hardest heart; and cowardice itself would have been induced, from her representation, to afford her that protection and support, which she declared was denied her by those, whose duty and interest it is to defend her.

The regret which Lockhart expressed at having seen Mrs Lee arose from the purest philanthrophy, founded on a belief that Mrs. Lee was an injured and virtuous woman.

Mrs. Lee did not venture to make a future appointment in Lockhart's presence, which she never failed to do both before and after that visit. Remark the ingenuity with which she contrived to draw me again to her house,—on Sunday, the 1st of January, she sent me some comments upon my Interpretation of her Dream, in a letter concluding with the following words:

" The natural attraction which we feel towards those whom we have known in the days of childhood, induces me to express a wish to see you in the course of next week."

The attraction which Mrs. Lee felt for me, was, I have no doubt, natural enough; and very naturally she described it, on Sunday, the 8th of January, the day appointed by herself for me to visit her. I will not more than once disgust the Public with an account of what passed on that morning, and shall only remark that I was induced to call again upon Mrs. Lee at eleven o'clock of the same night: she was in bed. When I called upon her on the next day, Davidson, her female servant, put a note into my hands, containing the following words.

"I cannot possibly see you unless I receive an apology."

I carried a flaming apology to Mrs. Lee in the evening, (Monday, the 9th of January.) The effect which it produced will be described in the following Narrative. On that night she shewed me a passage in her own hand writing, containing, to the best of my recollection, the following words.

"It is my determination to pass the remainder of my life in the society of a male companion; and with him to follow the plan of a Sect in Germany, who lead a monastic life, with the exception of celibacy."

I leave it to an impartial Public to affix epithets to the name of a married woman, who, after having shewn such a passage as that above-mentioned, to a young man, with whom she had previously agreed to elope, endeavoured to deprive him of his life and character, by swearing that her elopement was against her inclination.

On Wednesday, the 11th of January, I received a letter from Mrs. Lee, which is given at length in the narrative. It appears, at first sight, to be an argument against her elopement, which had previously been determined upon; but when the following extracts are compared with Mrs. Lee's determination, which she had before avowed, " to pass the rest of her life with a male companion," any unbiassed person must be convinced, that letter was merely intended to draw an answer from me, and to implicate Lockhart in the elopement, both which objects it unfortunately accomplished.

" My *determination* is *fixed*, and those who will not *second* it, are no friends of mine; shew this letter to your brother, and believe me to be, &c."

If Mrs Lee's determination was already fixed not to elope with me, what necessity was there for letting Lockhart know that such an improper scheme had ever been in agitation. The former part of the letter discovers Mrs. Lee's motive for wishing my brother to second the elopement:

" Neither your *age* nor your *situation* in life, are such as to afford me that *protection* and *support* which will be *necessary*."

And therefore she asked Lockhart in the plainest, as well as the most artful terms, whether he would unite his protection and support to mine. Lockhart's answer to Mrs. Lee, together with my own, are given in the annexed Narrative. I will not attempt to justify either· my own was dictated by that spirit of infatuation which irresistibly hurried me beyond the bounds of prudence and of virtue, and by incessant importunity I induced Lockhart to become an accessary to my own and Mrs. Lee's guilt.

On Thursday, the 12th of January, I called upon Mrs. Lee; the subject of conversation was our elopement, which she promised to undertake speedily; and desired me to ask Lockhart to dine with her on Sunday, that we might talk over and complete the plan. What must the world think of a married woman, who is capable of asking two brothers to dine at her house, and who put off her dinner an hour beyond the usual time, in order that the plan of her elopement might be circumstantially arranged? The Public will naturally expect that some reason for the elopement should be assigned; Mrs. Lee herself gave the reason: " Do you mean to live with me in this house? If you do, you cannot, my husband resides within two streets of me." Well, but what could induce her to make such a furious bustle, if she really wished and intended to go? " Aye there's the rub."

Davidson, her female servant, had lived twelve years (according to her own statement on the Trial) in Mr. Lee's family, previously to her entering Mrs. Lee's service, and was, as Mrs. Lee more than hinted, a spy of Mr. Lee's. It was equally dangerous to discharge her, or to let her into the secret. Mrs Lee, with her usual ingenuity, chose the middle course, and preserved her character with Davidson, whilst she gratified her wishes in eloping with me. Had Mrs. Lee seriously intended not to complete her promise, she had ample time and opportunity to escape from the house, or to procure the whole police of London for her protection. One convincing proof that Mrs. Lee might easily have procured the assistance of the very watchmen who took Lockhart into custody on the following night, is, that not more than five minutes elapsed from the time that Lockhart stopped in the hackney coach, at Mrs. Lee's door, on Monday night, the 16th of January, before he was surrounded in Clarges Street by an hundred people. If Mrs. Lee was really alarmed at the sight of Lockhart's pistol, what could induce her to tell her man-servant to desire him to come into the drawing room? Why did she not mention her being alarmed to the man-servant, when he carried candles to Mrs Lee in the drawing room?

Before Mrs. Lee left the eating room, Lockhart desired her to go up stairs, to dress herself in her riding habit, and put together whatever linen would be absolutely necessary for her journey. When Mrs. Lee left the eating room, she went into her bedchamber, no doubt with an intention of following Lockhart's advice, but on finding Davidson there, on her coming up stairs, Mrs. Lee found it necessary to act the farcical part which is detailed in the evidence given by Davidson on the Trial. Davidson has sworn that Mrs. Lee was very low during the whole of Sunday. I will not positively assert the cause of her more than usual depression of spirits before dinner, but I assert, without fear of contradiction from Mr. Edmonds, who is the respectable master of the Inn, at Tetsworth, and who waited upon Mrs Lee, during the whole time of supper, that few women have ever such a flow of spirits, as she appeared to have on Sunday evening.

Mrs. Lee's refusal to take any clothes with her, was the necessary consequence of her determination not to entrust Davidson with her secret. and her not taking

any money may be most happily accounted
for, by her having declared to me some
days before, that she had none, nor should
have any until the beginning of February.

Much, I am told, has been said about
my being in debt and that it was impossible for me to remain in London another
day.   It is not my wish, if it were in my
power, to deny the fact of my having been
compelled to contract debts which I am at
present unable to pay.   I was seven long
years in the army, six of which I passed in
various parts of the West Indies and the
British Settlements in America, where it is
well known that every article of consump-
tion is double, and frequently three times
the price at which it can be procured in
this country. I was compelled once, during
that period, to return to England, and
once to go to America, for the recovery
of my health, at my own expence.   I was
confined three months at Bellise, in the
Bay of Honduras, by a dreadful and ex-
pensive illness, the terrible effects of a
Coup-de-soleil   When it is known that I
never received the smallest pecuniary assistance from any one of my relations, I

debt contracted in the West Indies, long before I took the benefit of the Insolvent Debtors Act; but which I was compelled to give a note of hand for, in Jamaica, payable in London, in December last, by a threat of immediate imprisonment on my arrival in this country. Had I then been aware of the illegality of that threat, I should certainly not have given the note, much as I wished to discharge the claim. The sum of fifty eight pounds is due to the Captain of the ship, who brought me to England. I owe the remainder to my Taylor. It appeared to me to be absolutely necessary, that I should lay the above detail before the public, as many infamous falshoods are, I am informed, in circulation with respect to my character. General Churchill, who kindly appeared as an evidence on my trial, expressed his opinion of my conduct as an officer and a gentleman to several persons at Oxford, with the warmth of a real friend and the liberality of a perfect gentleman.

To return to the immediate object of this publication. It is worthy of remark that the moment Mrs. Lee walked out of

her house, being no longer in dread of
what her servants might say, she threw of
all restraint, by laughing so loud, that the
post boy who drove her to Uxbridge was
able to swear that he heard her.   Lord
Stair's coachman has declared that he could
and would have stopped Mrs. Lee, had
there been the smallest reason to imagine,
from her conduct, that any compulsion
had been made use of.   Mrs Lee was so
collected immediately after her getting into
the post chaise, as to ask Loudoun whether
he had shut the door   no doubt Mrs. Lee
asked that question for fear (as it actually
happened) that her servants should endeavour to prevent her elopement.

As to Lockhart's saying "drive on or I
will shoot you,' the post boy swore that
gentlemen very frequently said so to
him   and indeed it is a bad expression
which Lockhart has acquired by his being
in the habit of sporting, added to a natural
warmth of temper.   Before Mrs. Lee reach-
ed Tyburn Turnpike. she desired Lockhart
to observe how perfectly collected she was.
What in the name of good fortune could
possibly prevent her being so?   She well

knew the necessity there was to intimidate the servants, and to make them believe that she was really forced out of her house; and to do them justice, as far as their evidence can go, they have endeavoured to convince the world of the truth of their assertions.

The only evidence Mrs. Lee's Counsel had to produce in support of the charge against my brother and myself, were Mrs. Lee's own servants. To prove how impartial they were, I have evidence to substantiate that one servant swore on Sunday evening, after Mrs. Lee's elopement, that "they would hang them" (meaning my brother and myself) "if possible."

I have again to apologize for quitting the subject; the post boy drove us well, but Mrs. Lee's wishes far outstripped the legs of the horses; before we had gone five miles on the Uxbridge road, I felt her fumbling about my fingers and could not imagine what she could be doing. She discovered the ring which I had offered to her after dinner, upon my hand; she took it off; I conjectured her intention, and was in the act of putting it upon the

fourth finger of her right hand, when she
laughed and said "you do not know your
right hand from your left" and gave me her
left hand, upon the fourth finger of which I
put the ring.   One of the serious charges
against my brother, is, that he had prophaned
the sacred right of marriage, by desiring me
to present a ring to Mrs. Lee.   If he really
desired me to give that ring to Mrs. Lee with
a view of ridiculing or superseding her previous
marriage, he is either a fool or a madman;
and is equally entitled to commiseration.   I
offered that fatal ring to Mrs. Lee as a token of
that eternal love and friendship for her, which
I then vowed, and must for ever feel.   At the
moment Lockhart presented the ring to Mrs.
Lee, he gave way to his feelings, without
consulting his reason; he consented to the
gratification of a passion he had then much
reason to believe was sincere.   The return
which she has made to Lockhart is such as
he deserved, and such as, had he known the
whole of her conduct, he would have expected. — Women who have once forfeited

their characters, know that there is no reprieve in this world from the severe sentence which is passed against them, and which for ever drives them from the society of the virtuous and independent: careless of their present and hopeless of their future fate, they stalk abroad; and like painted sepulchres, are at once the pest and ornament of the city that contains them.

I shall make no further comment upon Mrs. Lee's denial, during her cross examination on the Trial, of her having accepted the ring. Mrs. Lee had previously sworn that she refused the ring, when first offered to her, and probably thought that it would appear like something more than inconsistency if she acknowledged her having voluntarily taken it from me in the post chaise.—Mrs. Lee confessed, during her cross examination, that she took her steel necklace from her neck, to which a small bag of camphor was attached. " it was her charm against pleasure." If proof were wanted of the folly, not to say the madness of infidelity, it might be fairly adduced, from Mrs. Lee's having declared that she does not believe in the truth of Christianity, and yet she supposes that *a small bag of camphor* can restrain those passions which the Great Author of our Being has given us for the wisest and most beneficent purposes, together with reason to govern them.—Mrs. Lee admits the credibility of her own dreams, the natural effect of indigestion; yet she affects to disbelieve the truth of those miracles and prophecies which have, for ages, convinced the best and wisest of mankind —Infidelity will believe any thing but the Bible —It has been very generally supposed that Mrs. Lee's confession of her having thrown away her necklace put an end to the Trial, the fact is otherwise, as will be seen by a perusal of Mrs. Lee's cross examination.

Mrs. Lee swore, on her examination before the Magistrates in Bow Street, that she was nearly in a state of insensibility during the whole of her journey to Tetsworth, and on the Trial she softened it down to her being panic struck. What Mrs. Lee's ideas may be of insensibility and being panic struck, I will not venture to determine, but I must be allowed to say, that she frequently gave me greater proofs of sensibility in the post chaise, than Lockhart wished, or could prevent, by any thing he said —When Mrs. Lee arrived at Tetsworth, she became extremely facetious, and asked me whether in my great coat, which she had on, " she did not look like a soldier's trull "

Before supper Mrs. Lee asked for egg wine, which appears to be her favourite liquor. As Mrs. Lee believes that *camphor* can perform one sort of miracle, she probably supposes that an *egg* can perform wonders of another kind. She discarded one charm because she had no further use for it; and lost no opportunity, during the rest of our journey, of shewing her devotion to a new one. Unfortunately there was only one egg in the house that night, Mrs. Lee eat that. I rather think the charm consists in the number of eggs which any one may eat, for I observed that Mrs Lee eat more every succeeding day than she had done the day before.

Next morning Mrs. Lee had breakfasted

and written her letter to Davidson, before Lockhart and myself were dressed. When we came down stairs we found Mrs Lee in a gown which Mrs Edmonds had kindly lent her, until her own was washed; she was a most ridiculous figure; Lockhart smiled which very much encreased her ill-humour Much unpleasant altercation passed, and Lockhart in vain endeavoured to convince her that she had no cause to be alarmed at his returning to London.

Soon after Lockhart left Tetsworth Mrs. Lee sent for Mrs Edmonds, the mistress of the Inn, into her bedchamber, and told her that " she had been forcibly brought from her house in London, by the two young men who came with her." Mrs Edmonds commiserated her situation, and told her she should be happy to render her any assistance; adding, " I suppose, Madam, you will not go any farther."—" O yes," answered Mrs. Lee, " I shall go on."

Mrs Lee's letter to Davidson is a masterpiece of art, she was afraid that Davidson might suspect the truth from her having made no resistance in London; and therefore wrote to her the following words, to convince Davidson of her innocence:

"No money, no clothes, death or compliance."

Davidson knew as well as Mrs. Lee that she had neither money nor clothes; and Mrs. Lee swore, on her Trial, that no sort of personal violence was at any time used towards her. The letter is equally absurd and false; had she wished for assistance, Mrs Edmonds would have procured it for her at Tetsworth; had she wished Davidson to know where she was going to, she would have told her. If Mrs. Lee had not acted with duplicity and treachery towards my brother and myself, she would have deserved, and no doubt would have excited universal compassion; her situation was dreadful in the extreme, there being no alternative left her, between the resignation of her fortune and reputation to the mercy of a husband she detests, or her endeavouring to convict me.

And here I think it my duty to exonerate
Lockhart from the charge of his having compelled me to go to bed with Mrs. Lee against
my inclination, by saying, when I was in his
bed-room, " if you do not get out of the room
I will shoot you." It is true that Lockhart did
make use of words to that effect; it was past
five o'clock in the morning; Lockhart was
tired and wanted to go to bed, but he certainly
was not so anxious to get me out of his room
as I was to go. I was longer undressing
myself than usual; Lockhart was impatient
and turned me out of his room without my
dressing gown; the chamber-maid, who was
in the room during the whole time, would
have sworn that what Lockhart said was not
spoken seriously.

Mrs. Lee was highly delighted with the
shawl which I purchased for her at Oxford,
and I have been informed she actually wore
the veil I gave her at Oxford, and only took it
off on her coming into Court.

At North Leach Mrs. Lee drank freely of
her favourite beverage, *egg wine*; we slept in

different beds, but Mrs Lee invited me in the morning to share her's, which I readily complied with

Tuesday, the 17th of January, at breakfast, Mrs Lee eat several eggs, we arrived safely at Gloucester, went to bed merrily, and on Wednesday morning Mrs Lee eat a more than usual quantity of eggs She was very anxious for Lockhart's arrival, and appeared to think that some accident had certainly befallen him; as she had dreamed that part of his skull was blown away

When Miller, the Bow Street Officer, made his appearance, Mrs Lee either was overwhelmed with sorrow and despair, or she acted to admiration What Mrs Lee's opinion of such a measure then was, may be discovered by her saying that "it was a base and unwarrantable liberty which had been taken with her, by sending a Bow Street Officer to take her and Loudoun into custody

During the time of dinner, at Gloucester Mrs Lee reprobated the circumstance of a Bow Street Officer having been sent to apprehend me, in the strongest terms. Mrs Lee gave such convincing proofs of her feelings, that Miller said, in the kitchen of the Inn at Tetsworth, " She loves him as she does her own dear eyes. No one will suspect Miller of having too much of the milk of human kindness in his composition yet he was less hardened than others, and permitted us to make vows of eternal fidelity to each other in private Mis Lee has broken those vows, the awful period must arrive, when we shall have to answer for them at the bar of an unerring and just Judge. I trust that by sincere repentance and contrition for our past errors and crimes, we shall obtain that mercy which the world is neither inclined nor enabled to bestow.

During my confinement in the New Prison, Clerkenwell, Mrs. Lee sent me word by a mutual friend, that she intended to keep the promise which she had made to me at Ux-bridge. Mrs Lee made two promises to me at that place, the one was, that she would, if I wished it pass the remainder of her life with me, the other, that she would share my imprisonment, should it be continued, the only thing I have to thank Mrs Lee for, is her not having performed those promises.

Mrs Lee expressed her sorrow for my situation, to the same common friend, during my confinement in Tothill-fields Bridewell, and said that she " regretted extremely her inability to supply me with money, as her solicitor had distrained fifty pounds of her income to pay the expences of the Bow Street Officer, to Gloucester, and back again to London " It is some consolation to me that I have never received nor solicited any kind of favour or assistance whatsoever from Mrs. Lee.

I am aware that it is making a miserable apology for the many errors of this publication, to say, that the Printer has frequently waited until I have supplied him with a continuation of the manuscript. I was induced to publish a statement of my brothers conduct and my own to Mrs Lee, not from a wish to obtain literary honours, but from an anxious desire to confute the authors and retailers of the gross falshoods which have been circulated to our prejudice, with so much industry and success That I have failed in the execution, must be attributed to my want of ability, not to the weakness of my case   My brother went to London after his acquittal, with a determination to bear " the whips and scorns of outrageous fortune," rather than publish a line in his defence

This work appears before the Public under every disadvantage.   I regret that I have not been enabled to state my case with the minute accuracy which I should have done, had I not delayed writing it until three weeks after the Trial, when I found myself imperiously called upon to publish it, in consequence of the cla‧mour which has been raised against my bro‧ther and myself   I can most positively assert, that no one circumstance which is detailed in this publication, is either intentionally or actually falsified.

L. H. GORDON

Oxford Castle, April 7, 1804.

NARRATIVE.

LOUDOUN GORDON called upon Mrs. Lee, at her house in Bolton Row, for the first time after his return from the West Indies, about seven o clock on the evening of Wednesday, the 14th of December, 1803. William Martin, Mrs. Lee's man-servant, opened the door, and said that his mistress was not at home: Loudoun then asked for a card to write his name upon; whilst the man-servant was fetching the card, Mrs. Lee called from the drawing-room door and said, " William, who is that?' William Martin then asked Loudoun his name, and the servant replied to Mrs. Lee, " Mr Loudoun Gordon." Mrs Lee immediately said, " Let him walk up " Loudoun then walked up stairs into the drawing-room; the usual expressions of joy at meeting again were exchanged, after which the conversation became general · Mrs. Lee spoke feelingly of her misfortune in having married Mr. Lee, she made some severe comments upon his conduct, which from Mrs. Lee's description did not

D 2

much redound to his credit as a husband. Mrs Lee enquired kindly after Loudoun's mother, his sister, and Lockhart, and finding from Loudoun that Lockhart was in London, she earnestly expressed her desire to see him, and she requested Loudoun to communicate her wishes to Lockhart, and to endeavour to persuade him to call upon her with Loudoun at his next visit. Mrs Lee shed tears when she mentioned the death of Loudoun's late elder sister Caroline, and requested to see an elegant and affectionate letter which Caroline had written to Loudoun when in the West Indies, a few days previous to her death. Davidson, the female servant, was sent to fetch Mr Dashwood's picture (Mrs Lee's brother,) and the man-servant brought coffee with those exceptions no third person was in the room during this visit which lasted about two hours. When Loudoun rose to take leave of Mrs Lee, she requested him to call upon her again on Saturday, (the 17th of December) and which he promised to do. Loudoun then saluted Mrs Lee, which she cheerfully acquiesced in, and took his leave of her.

On Friday the 16th of December, Loudoun called upon Mrs Lee about one o'clock, was admitted by her man-servant, when Loudoun

went into the drawing-room Mrs Lee said,
" I did not expect you till to-morrow (Saturday,) and that I might have the pleasure of
seeing you, I have put off an engagement I had
for that day" Loudoun recollected that he
had anticipated the day of his visit and apologized to Mrs. Lee for so common an error
Mrs. Lee asked Loudoun whether he had communicated to Lockhart the wish she had expressed to see him; Loudoun told her that he
had, and that he would endeavour to persuade
Lockhart to come with him the next time he
called upon her. Mrs Lee expressed her hope
that Loudoun would succeed in bringing Lockhart to her house The conversation turned
upon books and antient poetical writers, Mrs
Lee said, that Anacreon was one of her favourite poets, though she disliked poetry in general,
Loudoun said that he had an excellent transla-
tion of the Odes of Anacreon and Sappho's
Fragments; which Mrs Lee expressed a desire
to see. Loudoun said she should have it to
read Mrs Lee requested Loudoun to read
Vaillant's Travels into the Interior of Africa,
and give her his opinion of those travels at his
next visit Loudoun left the two pamphlets
which he had promised Mrs Lee on the 14th
of December Mrs Lee told Loudoun that
she intended to have gone to Bath in a short

time, but that she had just resolved to defer her leaving London Loudoun rose to take his leave of Mrs. Lee, when she fixed upon Saturday, the 24th of December, for his next visit

On Saturday, the 24th of December, about one o'clock, Loudoun called upon Mis. Lee, according to her appointment; before he was seated, Mrs Lee said " I had a presentiment that your brother would not come with you, and I think that I know the reason, he has probably heard that my opinions are sceptical, and that I have made many enemies by having become a sceptick, which I suppose is the cause of his not accompanying you, however, you may tell him, if you please, if he will let me see him, that I will never introduce the subject of religion " Loudoun replied, " that he was not aware of Lockhart being acquainted that Mrs. Lee had imbibed sceptical opinions, and that he believed Lockhart to be too liberal in his sentiments to make that the cause of his not accompanying Loudoun to call upon her." Mis. Lee then said, " What is the reason then that Lockhart does not come with you?" Loudoun replied, " I am ignorant of his reasons, but I well know that he has a larger acquaintance than he can possibly visit." Loudoun told Mis. Lee his opinion upon Vaillant's

Travels, " that he had been amused in reading them, but that he should have been better satisfied if he had seen the cabinet of curiosities which Vaillant asserts he had collected in Africa, particularly as some doubt remained in Loudoun's mind as to the truth of Vaillant's assertions, which were at variance with former travellers in Africa."

Mrs Lee reminded Loudoun of his not having sent Anacreon and the other books Mrs Lee told Loudoun that " she had not been out of her house for two months " Loudoun perceiving the state of her mind, requested Mrs. Lee to use exercise and other recreation and proposed her going to see a pantomime, which is usually performed at Christmas. Mrs. Lee in some measure consented to go, but mentioned one obstacle which prevented her, and that was " the fear of being insulted at the theatre " after Mrs. Lee had stated in strong colours her " dread of insult," Loudoun offered to go with Mrs Lee to the theatre, and protect her. Mrs. Lee gave her approbation, and laughed. Mrs Lee mentioned her having had a dream, and if Loudoun would permit it, she would read it to him. she then read the dream hereafter inserted, and made some remarks upon its extraordinary nature, and said that " the time of her dreaming it was equally remarkable with the dream itself, having been a few days before the appearance of the late meteor," with which phenomenon Mrs Lee appeared to think her dream might have some connexion. Loudoun observing Mrs. Lee's anxiety upon the subject of her dream, said that "it would probably bear some kind of elucidation, and that if she would entrust him with the paper on which it was written, he would endeavour to suggest some rational interpretation of it." Mrs Lee consented to let him have the dream, provided that Loudoun would promise upon his honour to shew her hand-writing to no one, with the exception of Lockhart the promise being made, Mrs. Lee carefully erased her name from the bottom of the paper containing her dream, and gave it to Loudoun for interpretation. The rest of the conversation was general, no third person was in the room during this visit, which lasted about two hours· when Loudoun rose to take his leave of Mrs. Lee, she said that she still hoped to see Lockhart, and made an appointment of some future day for Loudoun's next visit He observed, " it was not customary with him to be confined to any particular day to visit his friends, and that in future he intended to call upon Mrs Lee occasionally."

The following is the dream which Mrs Lee
gave Loudoun Gordon to interpret

" At about three o clock in the morning, as
the Watchman afterwards informed me, and as
I guessed, I thought I looked towards the
South East and beheld the sun gloriously bright,
rising amidst clouds tinted with gold   I never
in my waking hours saw this phenomenon so
beautiful   Gazing on it, I thought I exclaimed 'it is but three o clock and quite dark in
our hemisphere, yet the sun is rising' that is
strange   As I was musing on this deviation
from the usual course of nature, I directed my
eyes towards the North East, and perceived
the moon pale and rather clouded, but on each
side were two luminaries like suns, which
gradually enlightened her, till all the three
bodies had the appearance of globes of fire.
While I was observing them with peculiar
delight, suddenly the most magnificent edifice
that the human imagination can form, raised
itself out of the three fiery orbs   Its columns
were immense and roughly studded, in the way
of fret work, with precious stones, the floor
was glassy, but the roof and upper parts were
so immensely high that I could not discern
them, the architecture was complicated, and I
had not time to analyze it, but never was my mind

so strongly impressed with the ideas of beauty, grandeur and power I was absorbed in deep meditation, when I opened my eyes and heard the Watchman call 'past three o'clock.' I had before mentioned the hour during my sleep, which is a very remarkable circumstance.'

The following is the interpretation which Loudon Gordon returned to Mrs Lee's fiction.

December 27, 1803

DEAR MADAM.

Before I submit my thoughts to you upon the subject of the dream which you have done me the honour to communicate to me, allow me to assure you Madam, that it is not my intention to enter the lists as a champion for the truth of christianity, which could gain nothing, and might be injured by my mistatement of those arguments, or misapplication of those evidences which certainly deserve our most serious consideration.

" The sun rising gloriously bright in the South East," exactly represents the first appearance of Jesus Christ in Judæa. He is frequently stiled "the Sun of Righteousness," "the Light of the World," and "the the true Light." " The clouds tinted with gold," pourtray the mental darkness and error which at that time, *with some few exceptions*, degraded the whole human race The "moon in the North East" exhibits the first promulgation of the Gospel, the North being the quarter of the globe always first named, may figuratively express the beginning of any thing; "the moon being pale and rather clouded" alludes to the temporary humiliation and sufferings of the Great Author of our religion. "The two luminaries, like suns on each side of her," are the Father and the Holy Ghost. "The gradual illumination of the Moon" shews the progress of the great work of the redemption of mankind in the person of Jesus Christ, after the completion of which, our Saviour ascended into heaven and became one of the "three globes of fire." "The globes of fire' most happily illustrate the only idea we can form of the Trinity; fire having been allowed to be in all ages the purest symbol of the deity "The peculiar delight which you felt at observing" such glorious objects, is the natural effect upon the human mind, arising from the contemplation of the wonderful works of God "The magnificent edifice which raised itself out of the three fiery orbs" is Christianity "The immense columns" are the cardinal virtues; "their being roughly studded in the way of fret work" marks the difficulty of persevering in a virtuous course of life amidst the temptations and miseries of this world "The precious stones" strikingly pourtray the innate beauty of virtue. "The glassy floor' beautifully symbolizes the tranquillity and serenity of mind, which accompanies the true disciples of Christianity "The roof and upper parts of the edifice being so immensely high that you were unable to discern them, shews us the weakness and absurdity of our endeavouring to scan the ways of Providence, or to weigh the councils of omnipotence in the balance of poor human reason No wonder Madam that ' the architecture" of the great fabrick of revealed religion should have appeared "complicated" to you, and that "you should not have had time to analyze' those mysteries which "angels desire in vain to know, and which "the devils believe and tremble.'

It is impossible to consider the doctrines of Christianity without being impressed as you were with the highest ideas, of which the human mind is susceptible of "the beauty, grandeur, and power' of the great author of our existence.

That frequent meditation upon this, of all

other, most important subjects, may tranquillize your mind and make you as superior to the calamities which human nature is heir to, as your abilities are to the far greater part of mankind, is the sincere wish of, Dear Madam,

Your most faithful Servant,

L H Gordon.

P. S Lockhart presents his respects to you Madam, and hopes that you will see him on Friday Morning next, when he proposes to do himself the honour of calling upon you.

I take the liberty of returning the paper which you did me the honour to entrust to my care.

Lockhart and Loudoun Gordon called upon Mrs Lee about One o'Clock on Friday the 30th of December After the usual ceremonies which take place of course between old acquaintance who have not met for many years, Lockhart paid Mrs Lee some common-place compliments upon her good looks. After some indifferent conversation, Lockhart observed that he had been angry at not having his boots properly cleaned that Morning Mrs Lee said "what are you ever angry, and you too who are a Christian? She added " I am sure that I of all others ought to believe in a God. for I am quite astonished how I have been supported, having suffered every, even pecuniary distress." Mrs Lee asked after Lockhart's mother Lockhart said that she was well. Mrs Lee replied "I am happy to hear it. for she is a most wonderful woman, but I think her principles are too rigid, do not you think so?" Lockhart replied, "I think it impossible that any principles can be too rigid with regard to virtue."

Mrs. Lee gave a most disgraceful account of the conduct towards her of those who by all laws of God and nature ought to be her protectors, and which excited pity in Lockhart and Loudoun, as it must have done in any man who had heard the story which she then related. Mrs Lee reminded Lockhart of former days, and said that "he used to call her Dash when she resided at his mother's, and thunder at her door and say Dash! I will come in," Mrs. Lee said "she used generally to open the door". Lockhart said that "it had often given him pain when he recollected how roughly and in how school-boy like a manner he had treated Miss Dashwood at that time.' Mrs. Lee said "you did not treat me ill, I always took it as a mark of your affection, I thought you a fine, generous, open hearted boy." Nothing else material passed, Mrs. Lee said "she should always be very happy to see Lockhart" Lockhart observed to Loudoun, after having taken leave of Mrs. Lee, that he "regretted having seen her, and was sorry for her unhappy situation, and that he would not on any account, now he had renewed his acquaintance, have Mrs. Lee suppose that he treated her with neglect, and that he should therefore leave his card at her house occasionally."

On Sunday Night the 1st of January, 1804. when Loudoun returned home, he found a parcel containing two books which he had lent to Mrs. Lee, and the following letter.

January 1, 1804.
Your interpretation to the dream is replete with ingenuity and good sense; the former abounds when you launch into the regions of fancy, the latter predominates when you confine yourself to probabilities. And here let me caution you against giving scope to "mimick fancy," which often whilst she flatters your vanity, and amuses your mind, is leading your senses astray

The epithet of "the Sun of Righteousness,"

though not new, is exceedingly beautiful, alluding no doubt to that person who certainly was a light to some of his followers, who for the most part were vicious and ignorant. Some of the early mystical writers have termed him "the Day spring." I am much pleased with your remark upon "the immense columns." Your observation upon "the precious stones" is beautiful. The illustration of "the glassy floor" is very happy. I am fully convinced that virtue is congenial to the human mind, but in the present state of the world, the practice of it is attended with difficulty. I say in the present state of the world, for the serenity which accompanies virtue is so persecuted as almost to render it unattainable.

Vain indeed! is our attempt to scan the ways of Providence, "the immense fabrick" has been adapted by its wise author for purposes only known to himself.

The natural attraction which we feel towards those whom we have known in the days of childhood, induces me to express a wish to see you in the course of next week, with sincere good wishes, I subscribe myself,

Yours truly,

F. A. Lee

The parcel containing the books and the above letter, was sealed with red wax, the seal bearing the impression of the Anchor of Hope.

In consequence of Mrs. Lee's request, Loudoun called upon her on Monday the 2nd of January, 1804, about one o'clock, Sarah Hunt, the female servant, who opened the door, told Loudoun that Mrs Lee was gone to Hammersmith, Loudoun left word that he should call the following day. On Tuesday Morning the 3d of January, Loudoun called upon Mrs Lee about one o'clock, Mrs. Lee came to Loudoun in the dining room from the drawing room, and apologized for not having it in her power to remain with him that morning, an unexpected visitant having called upon her on particular business, and Mrs. Lee said if Loudoun would come on Thursday next, she should take care to be disengaged. Mrs. Lee said "I was going to write you a note not to come to day, but I feared you would not receive it early enough to prevent it." Loudoun took his leave of Mrs Lee and said that she might expect him on Thursday.

Loudoun being otherwise engaged on Thursday, wrote the following note to Mrs. Lee.

E

Mr Loudoun H Gordon presents his respects to Mrs. Lee, he is extremely sorry that the unfavourable state of the weather should have prevented him from having the honour of calling upon Mrs Lee this morning. which he hopes she will forgive Mr. Gordon proposes calling upon Mrs Lee on Sunday morning next

Thursday, January 5, 1804.

On Friday Loudoun received the following letter by the post from Mrs Lee.

DEAR SIR

I was much surprized at not having the pleasure of your company this morning, which I expected I shall be at home both on Sunday and Monday next, and shall be happy to see you upon either of those days.

I am,

Dear Sir,

Yours truly

F A Lee.

January 5 1804

This letter was sealed with red wax, the seal bearing the impression of the Anchor of Hope.

On Sunday morning, the 8th of January,

about one o'clock, Loudoun called upon Mrs
Lee, she complimented Loudoun upon his interpretation of her dream, some conversation
about dreams was started by Mrs Lee, Loudoun
said, " that Mrs. Lee's dream, from the circumstance of its being a morning dream, must,
according to the antient poets, be a true
one. '

" Post mediam noctem cum somnia vera "
Horace

Loudoun reminded Mrs Lee of some beautiful lines on the pleasure arising from dreams
in Ovid's Epistle from Sappho to Phaon, as
Mr Pope had translated it, beginning

" O night, more pleasing than the brightest day,
When Fancy gives what absence takes away,
And drest in all its visionary charms,
Restores my fair deserter to my arms " &c

Loudoun said that Brutus was probably
sleeping when the phantom which is said to
have called itself his evil genius, appeared to
him Loudoun asked Mrs Lee whether she
ever heard of Alexander's dream, Mrs Lee
begged Loudoun to relate it He said, " that
Alexander had a remarkable dream before he

undertook the conquest of Persia, a phantom habited in the dress of the Jewish High Priest, having appeared to him during sleep, and assured him of success. When Alexander approached Jerusalem, the High Priest, followed by many others, went out to meet him, and to implore the clemency of the Conqueror, who prostrated himself before the High Priest, and then Alexander related his dream ' Loudoun added, that "Augustus paid so much deference to dreams, that he was not indifferent to what others dreamed about him " Mrs Lee seemed to agree with Loudoun, that it was not impossible that dreams might be sent us for useful purposes

Mrs Lee said, " Loudoun, I have something very particular to communicate to you," Loudoun asked her what it was, Mrs Lee said, " that she thought it right to caution Loudoun in time against becoming enamoured of her; she therefore requested Loudoun, whenever he came to see her, to suppose that she was old and ugly, that she was unconscious of being either, and therefore it was the more likely that as Loudoun was young, he might be ensnared by her attractions '

Loudoun, who had long conceived an affec-

tion for Mrs Lee, replied, " that her caution
he had no doubt was intentionally good, but
happily he hoped for himself it was too late, as
his happiness was already in her hands, that
from his childhood he had ever retained a peculiar penchant for Mrs Lee, he called to her
remembrance some of their childish endear-
ments, and ended by saying that he had accounted that one of the most unhappy days of
his life on which he heard of Mrs Lee's marriage, which had placed the object of his af-
fections into the arms of another." Mrs Lee
asked Loudoun "how he had become acquainted
with the circumstance of her marriage," and said
that "he was too young to have conceived any
other than a childish affection for her, when
they had formerly lived together at his mother's.'
Loudoun replied, that "the affection which he
conceived for, and expressed to Mrs Lee in his
earlier days, was unalterable" Mrs Lee then
acknowledged that her affection for Loudoun
was reciprocal, and that " she loved him."
Mrs. Lee said, " what is it you propose to
yourself," leaning at the same time over the
table, and taking hold of one of Loudoun s
hands, " do you wish to live with me in this
house? if you did wish it, you could not, for
my husband resides within two streets of me."
Loudoun replied, " he had fixed on no positive

plan · and at that time arose from his chair, and frequently saluted and embraced Mrs Lee. Mrs. Lee appeared pleased at this, and it was evident that Loudoun and Mrs Lee had a mutual affection for each other, which it was equally the wish of both to indulge. Mrs Lee asked Loudoun "what the world would say if an union between them was to take place?" Loudoun replied in the language of Pope—

" Love free as air at sight of human ties,
   Spreads its light wings, and in a moment flies "

Mrs Lee said, " So you really wish me to become your pretty little mistress?" Loudoun replied, " human ties forbid you to be any thing else at present than the mistress of my soul " Some other conversation passed on this subject, which is immaterial.

Mrs Lee asked Loudoun if he had ever read Hawkins Browne's Poem on the Immortality of the Soul As Loudoun had not read it, she produced a manuscript in her own hand-writing, with some extracts from that poem, and which she begged Loudoun to read to her, after having read some lines, she told him, if he wished it, to take the extracts home, and read them at his leisure. Loudoun then arose and wished

Mrs Lee good morning, after having saluted her · he had been with Mrs. Lee without any third person being present about two hours · she appointed some future day for him to call.

About eleven o'clock the same night, the 8th of January, 1804, Loudoun rapped at Mrs. Lee's door, and the man-servant who opened it said, that his mistress was gone to bed. Loudoun intended to have seen her, but finding that she was in bed, left word that he should call in the morning.

On Monday morning, the 9th of January, about twelve o'clock, Loudoun called upon Mrs. Lee, at her house in Bolton Row; Davidson, the female servant, who opened the door to Loudoun, put into his hands the following note from Mrs. Lee.

" I can only attribute the rash action which you committed last night to intoxication, it is therefore impossible for me to see you until I receive an apology; indeed unless you intend to visit me as the friend of your infancy, perhaps it would be better, just at present, if you were to discontinue all personal intercourse."

In consequence of this note Loudoun did not express a wish to see Mrs. Lee.

In the evening of the same day, Loudoun returned to Mrs. Lee's house, between seven and eight o clock, and gave to her man-servant who opened the door, the following letter for Mrs. Lee, the servant said his mistress was very unwell, and would not be able to see any one.

9th January, 1804.

DEAR MADAM,

You do me justice by attributing the rash action which I unhappily committed last night to intoxication ! ! ! to intoxication of my soul, Madam.—I dined at my brother's lodgings by myself, and drank no wine, as he was from home; but I had drank *too* freely in the morning of the most delicious potion which I shall ever taste, not to feel its effects, which will be fatal indeed, should they occasion your lasting displeasure.

Forgive, Madam, the only action of my life which shall occasion your anger; do not drive me to despair, do but see me, and treat me like a dog as I deserve. I am,

Dear Madam,
Your most wretched servant,
L H. GORDON.

As soon as Mrs. Lee had read this letter, she sent to request Loudoun to walk up stairs. When the servant had gone out of the drawing-room, Loudoun knelt down upon one knee, took hold of Mrs. Lee's hand, and looked earnestly in her face. Mrs Lee laughed at so tragi-comic an attitude. and said " Loudoun, it was not kind of you to call in the evening, why did you come so late? ' Loudoun seeing Mrs. Lee's good humour, and that his letter had been a sufficient apology, kissed her hand and arose. Loudoun could account for his conduct in no other way than by that expressed in his letter which she had just read A table at this time divided them; Mrs. Lee said to Loudoun " move your chair ' she at the same time moved her own, and the chairs in which Loudoun and Mrs Lee sat, came in consequence close together. After endearing salutations and embraces which frequently succeeded each other during three hours, the whole plan of elopement was matured by mutual consent. Loudoun proposed a journey into Wales; Mrs. Lee asked if " he meant to take her to a Welch inn," the thought of which she appeared to dislike · he replied that "he would endeavour to procure a cottage for her " Mrs Lee said "she hoped that Loudoun would succeed," he asked her whether she meant to take her servants with her. Mrs Lee said, "Oh, no! I can travel without servants, and we can procure Welch servants when we are at our journey s end" Mrs. Lee said, ' that the elopement must be contrived without the knowledge of her own servants, especially as Davidson, the female servant, had lived in Mr. Lee's family," who, Mrs. Lee hinted, was a spy upon her conduct, and that she had taken Davidson out of Mr. Lee's family, to shew them that her conduct was such as not to fear the eye of scrutiny

Little did Mrs. Lee then imagine that I should ever know so much of her prior conduct as has since unhappily for myself come to my knowledge.   Loudoun asked Mrs Lee whether she intended to retain her present establish-ment when she left London, Mrs Lee said, " that she was paying two hundred and fifty pounds a year for her house in Bolton Row, and that, as well as the servants, would be an unnecessary expence ' Mrs Lee then took a book bound with morocco leather and which had steel clasps, when opened, Loudoun ob-served it to be partially filled with her own hand-writing. Mrs Lee looked for a particu-lar passage, and pointed out to Loudoun the following words " It is my determination to pass the remainder of my life in the society of a male companion, and with him to follow the plan of a sect in Germany, who lead a monastic life, with the exception of celibacy.' After Loudoun had read that passage, she said " you see how unnecessary it will be to keep this house and my servants, and therefore it would be better to discharge them, with the exception of Sarah Hunt, my cook, who has been with me for six years, and to whom I am much attached ' Mrs Lee expressed her dislike of Davidson. The plan about the house, and servants, being so far arranged, it was agreed that the cook should remain to take charge of the house in Bolton Row during Mrs Lee's absence, until some definitive arrangement could be made Mrs Lee said that there was one material obstacle to the completion of their expedition, and that was, that ' she had no money, as her dividends would not become due until the ensuing month (February).' Loudoun removed that objection, by saying that " he had funds adequate to the purpose " Mrs. Lee seemed pleased at this information · Loudoun then proposed bringing a post-chaise to-morrow (Tuesday, the 10th of January), for the purpose of setting out for Wales Mrs Lee asked, " why he wished to be so precipitate," and said " you must have some presentiment of something evil about to befal me, by wishing to execute our elopement so hastily. ' Loudoun assured Mrs Lee that he had no such presentiment, and said, " that when he proposed an immediate elopement, he was convinced from her own confession, it was only what she herself wished, and that she had too much good sense not to lay aside dull forms and prudish ceremonies in the conclusion of an affair which was so intimately connected with their mutual happiness.' Mrs. Lee allowed the truth of Loudoun s observation, and promised to raise no obstacle to prevent the execution of the proposed scheme, but she said that "Loudoun must be aware of the difficulty of screening her consent to the elopement from her servants, and that she had some arrangements to make first, and that it would be necessary for her to consult a male friend about those arrangements." Mrs Lee described her situation to Loudoun, and which she depicted as being insupportable. Loudoun from her own description had every reason to suppose that she was very unhappy, and pointed out the propriety of her confiding in some male companion, upon whose bosom she could lay her head, and to whom she might impart the sorrows of her heart, which he said he had reason to fear were too bitter for her to bear, but which when divided into separate channels would alleviate the burthen that she was then ready to sink under. Mrs Lee fell upon Loudoun's neck and embraced him.

Mrs. Lee read Loudoun the construction which she herself had put upon the dream; it began in the following words "Some immediate and material change is about to take place in my situation" This change Mrs Lee said "could allude to nothing less than her union with Loudoun." the remainder of this interpretation he has forgotten, but Loudoun observed to Mrs. Lee that she had been kind enough to elucidate it very favourably to their mutual wishes.

Mrs Lee asked "what Loudoun's mother and Lockhart would think of their elopement ' " He replied, that he could not possibly tell ' Mrs Lee repeated several times during the evening, " What then you really wish me to become your little mistress?" the answer was invariably " the mistress of my soul, Mrs Lee."

Mrs. Lee said, " She was convinced that Loudoun's mother would highly disapprove of her conduct, and his too, when she heard of the elopement, and said that Mrs Gordon had the most unalterable opinions with regard to virtue; that she used sometimes, in order to teaze Mrs Gordon, to observe that "she (Mrs Lee) conceived there was no sin in the commission of fornication." Mrs Lee said that "Mrs. Gordon always rebuked her warmly, and ordered Mrs Lee to read instantly a certain chapter in the New Testament, denouncing punishment for the sin of fornication.'

Loudoun said, "that he wished before he left Mrs Lee, to have a promise that she would perform her intention of eloping, (as she said it was impossible for them to reside together in London,) and fix the day for that purpose; he requested that it should not be delayed beyond Saturday' Mrs Lee promised' to raise no obstacle in the way of the elopement, and that if Loudoun would give her until next Thursday (the 12th of January) to arrange every thing, she would upon that day fix a time for their leaving London' During the last three hours Mrs Lee's and Loudoun's chairs had been close together the intervals of cessation in conversation were filled up by mutual and warm embraces About eleven o clock, Loudoun rose to wish Mrs Lee good night, she presented Loudoun with her pocket handkerchief, and he gave Mrs Lee his own in return It is to be remarked that the handkerchief which Mrs. Lee gave to Loudoun was marked L 9 the

number nine is a perfect number, nine is also
a mystic number, representing perfection, and
no doubt alluded to Mrs Lee's perfect love and
submission to Loudoun, Mrs Lee has made
some proficiency in the knowledge of the ab-
struse sciences.

                   " that handkerchief
Did an Ægyptian to my mother give.
She was a charmer, and could almost read
The thoughts of people. She told her, while she kept it,
'Twould make her amiable, and subdue my father
Entirely to her love; but, if she lost it,
Or made a gift of it, my father s eye
Should hold her loathly, and his spirits should hunt
After new fancies She, dying, gave it me;
And bid me, when my fate would have me wive
To give it her I did so and take heed on't.
Make it a darling like your precious eye;
To lose't or giv't away, were such perdition
As nothing else could match.
        There is magic in the web."

   On Tuesday Afternoon Loudoun wrote the
following letter to Mrs Lee.

                    January 10, 1804
My DEAR MADAM,
         You have indeed put my
fortitude to the test by commanding me to

absent myself for two whole days from all that
is dear to me, in this instance, as in every other,
I shall submit myself to your better judgment
and discretion, fly, fly away ye sluggish hours,
that I may behold the only object in this world
worthy of my contemplation and adoration.

I entrust this letter to the penny post for
fear of exciting suspicion, where it may be
fatal.

> Think of me, and believe me to be,
> My dearest Madam,
> Your faithful and affectionate,
> L. H. Gordon.*

* Mrs Lee in her conversation with me on Monday
night the 9th of January, expressed her fear of what might
happen, meaning her dread of my being killed in a duel in
consequence of my elopement with her, she said that "she
should require the most ample protection." The time of
leaving London, independant of the above, is an additional
reason for having pistols. And let me ask the reader, male
or female, what man is so incautious as to elope with a
woman without pistols, and what married woman would
be willing to go, unless she had previous knowledge of his
having them for her protection?

As a proof that the elopement was agreed upon on Monday
night, the 9th of January, I lay before the public the following
memorandum, accompanying the present of a brace of pistols,
which Lockhart gave to me on Wednesday Morning the
11th of January.

On Wednesday Evening Loudoun received the following letter from Mrs. Lee.

"You have drawn a true and faithful picture of my situation, but you have pro-

"Let it be indelibly impressed on your mind, that the trifling present which accompanies this letter, was given you for the protection of your own honour, and the defence of an injured woman, who deserves your love, and commands your respect, by sacrificing every thing desirable in this world, for the sake of your society   Never argue, never dispute, avoid a first quarrel as you would a pestilence; sleep in different beds, never dress in the same room; observe the most scrupulous delicacy at all times and upon all occasions, enjoy, but do not abuse, the mystic rights of Venus.

Believe that this advice is given you from an earnest wish for your future happiness, and is the result of much observation.   This is the last time that I shall ever give you my advice unasked for——vive valeque."

Loudoun related the above letter to Mrs Lee, on Sunday night in the post chaise, when he repeated "by sacrificing every thing desirable in this world for the sake of your society," Mrs. Lee said "then you allow Lockhart that I sacrifice every thing for the sake of Loudoun's society." Lockhart answered, "Mrs. Lee you must depend on yourselves for society "

This letter is another convincing proof that it was not Lockhart's intention to participate in the elopement, had not Mrs Lee by her artful letter of the 11th, and invitation of the 12th of January, induced him afterwards to do so.

posed strange means of alleviating it By my
consenting to your proposal you will gain
much, and I shall lose the little which I still
possess, neither your age nor your situation
will be able to afford me that protection and
support which will be necessary. Consult your
heart consult your reason, and let me know
the result. If pleasure were my object, neither
my mind nor body are at present in a state
which would make the enjoyment of it desirable
to me You must be well aware of the opinion
which the world will form of you and me.
You say that you are my friend, prove it by
the sacrifice of a youthful passion When you
were a boy I perceived in you generous sentiments, let me see that time has not destroyed,
but matured them You say that you will
submit to my better judgment and discretion,
I now exact from you the fulfilment of your
promise My *determination* is fixed, and
those who will not *second* it are not my friends
Communicate this letter to your brother and
believe me to be,

Yours truly,

F A Lee.

January 11 1804

In consequence of the above, Loudoun
called upon Mrs. Lee with the two following
letters.

My Dearest Madam,

If you assent to my proposition, I shall gain an inexhaustible source of felicity; you will lose the pity of the ignorant and the prejudiced. The protection that I have to offer you Madam, is the strength of body and mind, the courage and the life of a man, not unused to danger. My age, Madam, has been matured by adversity, the only school of true philosophy, my situation, though it is not what I could wish, nor what my education and birth might have led me to expect, is rendered less irksome, by the possession and enjoyment of that inestimable treasure, mens conscia recti, which can neither be purchased nor stolen. I have consulted my heart, and would have plucked it out had it dared to think you less than the most perfect of human beings. I have consulted my reason in a low, but clear voice, it whispered praise Pleasure, name it not my heart, for I have found no traces of you imprinted there If the union of congenial souls can be rendered more complete by the union of their bodies, obey Madam the first mandate of God and of nature, or tremble at the thoughts of your disobedience The world Madam is unworthy of you, the false opinion which it will probably form with regard to your conduct, will never be able to shake your constancy or fortitude. In obedience to your commands I have communicated your letter to my brother, he respects, he admires you, and he says that he will protect you at the hazard of his life and fortunes I can feel, though I cannot express what I am to you, more than that I am,

My Dearest Madam,

Your sincere and affectionate,

L H. Gordon.

My Dear Madam,

I consent with all my heart to every thought, word and expression contained in Loudoun's answer to your letter, which you did me the honour to desire him to communicate to me If Loudoun deceives you Mrs. Lee, I will certainly blow his brains out, and then we shall both be eternally damned as we shall most richly deserve. Strong feelings burst the fetters of ceremony, and express themselves in the untutored language of nature Mrs Lee will find in Lockhart Gordon a friend who has a head to conceive, a heart to feel, and a hand to execute whatever may conduce to Mrs. Lee's happiness

I have the honour to be, &c.

L. Gordon

William Martin the man-servant immediately

that Mrs Lee had read the two letters, came into the dining room and said that his Mistress desired Loudoun to walk up stairs. Loudoun went into the Drawing Room and saluted Mrs Lee Mrs. Lee said that she had consulted the male friend she had spoken of to Loudoun, the last time he was with her, who had dissuaded her from eloping, in something like the following words "If you stand your ground you are acting a proper part, but if you take the step of elopement you will let the hell-hounds loose upon you" A good deal of conversation, which Loudoun has forgotten, then passed about the elopement, but it convinced him that Mrs Lee was as willing to undertake the expedition as she had expressed herself to be on the preceding Monday. Loudoun frequently saluted Mrs Lee, and once got up and shewed her the passage in the letter, beginning "If the union, which she did not attempt to refute Mrs Lee then requested Loudoun to go and see her picture at Mr Cosway's the painter before he next came to see her Loudoun said to Mrs. Lee "unless the elopement takes place soon, you must never expect to see me again" Mrs Lee promised that there was every probability that she should be able to go soon, and then invited Loudoun to dinner on the ensuing Sunday, and requested

him to get his brother Lockhart to accompany
him, and then they would talk over on that
day and settle the matter Upon this condition
Loudoun accepted the invitation, and when
Lockhart returned home from dining out the
same night, Loudoun told Lockhart of Mis Lee s
engagement After much persuasion Lockhart
consented to accompany Loudoun at dinner
with Mis Lee.

Loudoun wrote the following note on Thursday night to Mis. Lee.

My Dearest Madam,
                                Lockhart will do himself
the honour of accompanying me at dinner with
you on Sunday next at four o'clock.
        I have the honour to be,
                My dearest Madam,
                        Your most sincere and affectionate,
                                L. H. Gordon.
January 12, 1804.

On Sunday the 15th of January, between
four and five o'clock in the afternoon, Lockhart and Loudoun Gordon went to Mis Lee's
house in a hackney coach, and were admitted
by the man-servant, who announced them to
Mis. Lee in the drawing room, where she was
sitting with the window open, after the usual

expressions of civility, Lockhart asked Mrs Lee
if she usually sat with the window open at that
time of the year, she replied, that "she thought
it a very warm day," however Lockhart shut
the window, not being of so warm a constitution
as Mrs Lee Mrs Lee said to Lockhart "were
you not very much surprised at the communication Loudoun made to you?' Lockhart said
that "he was not surprised at any thing so
natural," he added 'we shall not have time
to discuss the subject before dinner, and had
therefore better defer it till afterwards' Mrs.
Lee said that 'she had ordered the dinner an hour
later on purpose that there might be time enough
for the discussion before dinner' Further
conversation about the elopement then took
place Mrs Lee said "that in a year Loudoun
would be running all over the town after
other women," Loudoun replied, "Your beauty
Madam is a sufficient security against that'
Lockhart said "I think the best thing you
can do is to go out of town in a post chaise
this evening' Mrs Lee laughed, the man
servant announced dinner, which put an end to
the conversation Loudoun handed Mrs Lee
down stairs to the eating room, the conversation
was general during the time of dinner Mrs.
Lee hobbed a nob, as it is vulgarly called, with
Lockhart, by placing the bottom of her glass

on the top of Lockhart's, and vice versâ; the same ceremony was repeated with Loudoun, and no doubt was symbolical of the union which it was then Mrs. Lee's intention to complete that night.

Some jests past during dinner, when the servant was absent, alluding to the state in which Mrs Lee and Loudoun had agreed to live in   Common place conversation took place after dinner, the bottle circulated pretty freely, about seven o'clock Lockhart took out his watch and said "the post chaise will be here presently," Mrs Lee asked what post chaise? Lockhart replied "the post chaise in which you and Loudoun are going into Wales" Mrs. Lee laughed in a girlish way, and said to Loudoun "is he in earnest?" Loudoun replied 'yes he is and I am glad of it, for we now shall be enabled to accomplish what we mutually wish, but want resolution to effect' Lockhart said "Loudoun you have a trifling present to give Mrs. Lee, come and fetch it" He went round the table and Lockhart gave him a ring, and told Loudoun to put it on Mrs Lee's finger, Lockhart said to Mrs Lee "it is the only pledge of affection which he now has it in his power to give you" Mrs Lee refused to accept the ring, Loudoun did not even press her to take it; the ring remained upon the table. Some conversation which has escaped Loudoun then took place, when Lockhart said, "we are fully prepared for the journey, for we have pistols for your protection" Mrs Lee then rose from her chair and felt Lockhart's pockets, he took out a pistol to prove the truth of what he said to Mrs Lee, and put it again into his pocket Lockhart requested Mrs Lee to put her riding habit on, and procure some linen which she would require on the journey, however Mrs Lee declined doing so Mrs Lee ran round the table and felt Loudoun's pockets, Lockhart desired Loudoun to go and see whether the post chaise was ready, when Loudoun went out of the room Mrs Lee wished to follow him; Mrs Lee went up stairs, after having rang the bell, which the man servant answered Loudoun in a few minutes came into Lockhart, and said the chaise was ready, Lockhart desired Loudoun not to leave Mrs Lee alone, but to go up to her into the drawing room, Loudoun as he went up stairs, heard Mrs Lee desire the man-servant to request Mr Lockhart Gordon to come into the drawing room Loudoun went to Mrs. Lee, who was kneeling upon a chair, with her face to the back of it, he saluted Mrs Lee repeatedly, and embraced her. Loudoun said "come Mrs. Lee there is no time to be lost, pray put on your habit and take those things which you will more immediately require" Mrs Lee said "I cannot go, I am not prepared" After some further conversation, in which Mrs Lee displayed that reluctance which was to be expected when the eyes of her servants were upon her, Lockhart came into the drawing room, and Loudoun said the chaise is ready Lockhart said "come Mrs Lee let us go" Mrs Lee then walked towards the door of the drawing-room, when she observed Davidson, the female servant coming towards her, and Sarah Hunt the cook. Davidson came and took Mrs Lee's hand and said "my Mistress shall not go out of her house," however Mrs Lee did go out, having walked very quietly down stairs, through the passage and into the post chaise, which was fifty yards from her door The two female servants made a great outcry, ignorant that their Mistress was a party concerned Lockhart took a pistol out of his pocket to prevent the foolish women making a noise, at which they were so alarmed that they neither knew what they did nor said As Loudoun and Mrs Lee were walking towards the chaise, they met a man, who afterwards proved to be Lord Stair's coachman to whom Mrs Lee said, "Who are you, do you know me?" She repeated the question and then turned to Loudoun and asked him whether he knew whom he was. Loudoun said he did not, and it did not signify. Mis Lee appeared to fear it might be a servant of some neighbour, who might recognize her. After they were in the post-chaise, she asked Loudoun whether he had shut the door of her house. Loudoun replied, "I left Lockhart there." He then looked out of the post-chaise door, and saw Lockhart coming from Mrs Lee's with Loudoun's great coat, so little did Lockhart think that Mrs. Lee was serious in the opposition which she affected to make in her house. As soon as Lockhart got into the chaise he told the post-boy to drive on, or he would shoot him; a phrase which Lockhart, from having been a great sportsman, is very apt to make use of. Mrs Lee's servants were at that time bawling out in the street, and Loudoun was fearful would obstruct Mrs Lee's intended elopement.

Before the post-chaise arrived at Tyburn Turnpike, Mrs. Lee said, "Do not I support my presence of mind wonderfully well?" The conversation then became general respecting the conduct of the servants. Mrs Lee said, "there was no fire in the drawing-room, and asked whether we had told her servants not to

make one there" Lockhart assured her "that
we had said nothing to any of them about the
plan of elopement' Mis Lee requested that
all the windows of the post-chaise might be up,
observing at the same time, "that as we were
all young, our breath would not be offensive to
each other' Loudoun sat next to Mrs Lee,
who before they had travelled far, embraced
Loudoun When they were about four or five
miles from London, Loudoun felt Mrs. Lee attempting to take the ring off his finger, which he
had before offered to her in the dining-room:
Loudoun took the ring from Mrs Lee, when
she had taken it off his finger, and was going
to put it upon the fourth finger of her right-
hand, when she said, "Pugh! you are going
to put it on the wrong hand," she took the
ring from Loudoun, and put it upon the finger
of her left hand, which is appropriated to the
marriage ring, and said ' In compliance with
the custom of the world I consent to wear this
ring Lockhart said, "I hope the ring fits
you, Mrs Lee?" She said, "Yes it does.
Lockhart replied, "it is a good omen" Mrs
Lee mentioned her having a ring up on her marriage finger, which represented a serpent with
its tail in the mouth

Immediately after M.s Lee had put the ring

upon her finger, Lockhart observed her letting down the window, and flinging something out of it; he asked, "What have you thrown away, Mrs Lee?" she replied, "My necklace, it has a bag of camphor suspended to it, which was my charm against sensual pleasure; but as I have no longer any occasion for it, do not you think that I am right in flinging it away" Loudoun replied, " certainly"

Lockhart said that he should return to London from Uxbridge that night. Mrs Lee then said, " it will be infamous in you if you do, as you have commenced the journey with us, you are in duty bound to continue it, the world will never forgive you for deserting us now' Mrs Lee would not hear of Lockhart's intention to return to London Lockhart replied, " I never intended to have gone with you, I have no cloaths, my presence is absolutely necessary in London, to consolidate my interest, which I am making for a living, and I must appear at a ball to-morrow night. Mrs. Lee said, " I suppose you intend to tell all the pretty misses at the ball that I have eloped with Loudoun. ' Lockhart said, " How can you suppose that I could be guilty of such an action, for my own interest you may be well assured of my silence on the subject. Mrs

Lee said, " I am sure you can go to London for no other purpose but to let it be known that I have eloped with your brother." Lockhart assured Mrs Lee that she was mistaken in her ideas altogether, that it was to his interest as well as hers that the world should be ignorant of the elopement. A long altercation took place between Lockhart and Mrs Lee, during which Mrs Lee insisted upon Lockhart's continuing the journey into Wales, which at length drew from Lockhart a promise that " he would remain with them that night, and although it would annihilate every prospect which he had in life, yet if she continued to insist upon it, he would go on with them into Wales, rather than Mrs Lee should have to accuse him of not consulting her happiness."

At Uxbridge, Lockhart went into the inn, where he staid about twenty minutes, Mrs. Lee and Loudoun remained in the post-chaise: she drank some porter, and when the other chaise was ready, it was at Mrs Lee's request drawn up so closely to the one they were in, that Mrs. Lee was able to step from one into the other: there were several people employed in changing horses and the baggage, Mrs Lee would not permit a lanthorn to be brought near the post-chaise for fear of being seen, which precaution she did not omit even at the turnpike gates She also particularly charged them both not on any account to name the word Lee, so little did she wish that her elopement might be known even in the post-chaise if the name of Lee happened to be mentioned by Lockhart or Loudoun, they met with a very severe rebuke, and to say the truth, Mrs. Lee used much more precaution than Loudoun, that they should not be traced by her husband. Lockhart proposed that Mrs. Lee should sleep at Wycombe, there being a good inn at that place· Mrs Lee expressed a wish to go a stage beyond Wycombe, and said " however happy I may be to-night, yet local circumstances will damp my pleasure at Wycombe," alluding no doubt to the residence of her reputed father, which was at West Wycombe.

Lockhart went to sleep, and when he awoke he observed, that Mrs Lee was toying with Loudoun. Lockhart said, " Well, I see that neither of you will be able to hold out beyond Wycombe, so you had better resolve upon sleeping there Mrs. Lee expressed a wish to go on to Tetsworth or Oxford that night

They changed horses at Wycombe, where nothing material happened Mrs Lee appeared very contented, and at one time went to sleep. At the

time we arrived at the inn at Tetsworth the mail
and Worcester coach were there, the people of
the inn were in bed. Mrs Lee was handed out of
the chaise by Lockhart and Loudoun supper was
ordered whilst Loudoun went to choose a bedchamber, and to see the sheets well aired, which
Mrs. Lee had particularly requested him to do in
the post-chaise. Mrs Lee wished much to have
some egg wine after supper, there were no eggs
in the house, the chambermaid asked Mrs. Lee
if she wished her bed made in any particular way·
Mrs. Lee said, " put the mattress on the top of
the feather-bed." Mrs. Lee eat a hearty supper;
the conversation during supper was on the intended use of the Pyramids of Egypt, on Grecian
architecture, and Hieroglyphicks Soon after
supper Mrs. Lee went to bed. About twenty
minutes after Mrs. Lee had gone to bed, Loudoun
rang the bell, and told the chambermaid to go
and see whether the lady wanted any thing, the
chambermaid returned and told Loudoun that the
lady said "she should be in bed in twenty minutes."
The chambermaid came into the room where Lockhart and Loudoun were sitting, Lockhart desired
her to be particularly attentive to Mrs Lee, in
consequence of which she again went to Mrs Lee,
knocked at the bed-room door, and asked her if
she could do any thing for her Mrs. Lee said,
" I am not in bed yet, but you may tell the gen-

tleman to come to bed in ten minutes." The chambermaid communicated Mrs. Lee's message to Loudoun. About forty minutes after Mrs. Lee went to bed, Lockhart rang the bell, and desired the chambermaid to warm his bed; he went up to his room and Loudoun with him. After they were in the bed-room, Loudoun sent the chambermaid for his portmanteau, and was a long time fumbling about the room, washing his teeth, &c. Lockhart wanted to go to bed, and said to Loudoun, " if you do not get out of the room I will shoot you." Loudoun wanted his dressing gown, Lockhart having had some experience of the warmth of Mrs. Lee's constitution in the post-chaise, told Loudoun that he ought to be ashamed of not going to bed, and turning to the chambermaid said, " Did you ever see a fellow make such a piece of work about going to bed to his own wife?" At last Loudoun went to bed. —The curtains were drawn.—

Monday, January 16th, Mrs. Lee had breakfasted before Lockhart and Loudoun came down. A long altercation took place between Mrs. Lee and Lockhart, in the course of which she called him a great scoundrel, for wishing to go to London, in order to amuse the pretty misses at the ball, he intended going to that evening, at her expence. Lockhart endeavoured to convince Mrs. Lee that he was obliged to return to London to make interest for a family living which was likely to become vacant. At last Mrs. Lee gave reluctant consent to Lockhart's returning to London, but still believed that Lockhart intended to expose her, which no doubt induced her to send the following letter to Davidson, her female servant.

" No money, no cloaths, death or compliance."

After Lockhart left Tetsworth, Mrs Lee went into her bed-room, rang the bell, and desired the chambermaid to send up the mistress of the house to her. Mrs Edmonds went to Mrs. Lee, who said, " Can I place any confidence in you?" Mrs. Edmonds answered that she hoped she might Mrs Lee told Mrs Edmonds that " she had been forced from her house in London by the two young men who came with her " Mrs. Edmonds expressed her sorrow for Mrs. Lee's unhappy situation, and offered her any assistance that she might choose to have, and every accommodation that it was in her power to afford her Mrs. Lee said, " Although you see me in this situation, you may be assured that I am a person of fortune and consequence, did you observe that gentleman who went away just now? Did he look like a clergyman?" Mrs. Edmonds replied, " that she did not observe the gentleman particularly, and most gentlemen wore their hair cropped, which made it difficult to distinguish a clergyman." Mrs. Lee asked whether Mrs. Edmonds had observed any thing singular in his appearance or manner? She said, "No, the gentleman looked grave." "He is mad (said Mrs. Lee) and very mad too." Mrs. Edmonds supposed that Mrs. Lee would not go any farther: "O yes, said Mrs. Lee, I shall go on," which put an end to the extraordinary conference. Mrs. Lee put on her own gown and stockings, having worn some belonging to Miss Edmonds whilst they were washed; she borrowed a shawl of Mrs Edmonds, and set out very readily with Loudoun for Oxford.

Lockhart desired Mrs. Lee to give him a note to her servants for her cloaths, which probably gave rise to a report of his holding a pistol in one hand and a draft in the other to Mrs. Lee for her signature, a thousand lies of the same tendency have been circulated with a view of rendering Lockhart's character infamous.

Lockhart left Tetsworth between two and three o'clock on Monday afternoon, Loudoun then asked Mrs. Lee at what time she wished to set out on their journey towards Gloucester, she replied "We had better dine here, and set out after dinner, I wish to travel as much as possible by night." After dinner, Mrs. Lee, as before related, went into her bedchamber to change her gown and stockings, which had been washed, where she staid about an hour, she came again into the room, where Loudoun was sitting, in apparent good humour. The post-chaise being ready, Loudoun handed Mrs. Lee into it about half-past four: nothing material happened till they arrived at the King's Arms Inn, Oxford, where they changed horses, and ordered the post-boy to drive to Mr. Randall's, haberdasher, in the High Street, where a straw-bonnet, black veil and shawl, were purchased according to Mrs. Lee's wish. Mrs. Lee would neither go into the shop to examine the articles, nor suffer Mr. Randall to bring a candle to the post-chaise that she might see them. The bill being paid they went as far as Northleach that night, having changed horses and the post-chaise at Witney. At the various turnpikes through which they passed, if the person who came for the toll brought a candle, Mrs. Lee expressed her anger, so anxious was she to travel unknown. Mrs. Lee desired Loudoun to choose a bed-chamber, and to see that the sheets were aired at Northleach. Mrs Lee eat very heartily at supper, and drank egg wine enough to compensate for her not having been able to obtain any on the preceding night at Tetsworth. During supper at Northleach, Mrs. Lee, wishing Loudoun and herself to be in private, told the servant-maid that she need not wait at table. About an hour after supper Mrs. Lee went to bed, when the chamber-maid told Loudoun that Mrs. Lee was gone to bed, he went into a separate bed in Mrs Lee's bedchamber. In the morning Mrs. Lee awoke Loudoun, and desired him to come into her bed, which summons he readily obeyed. They break-fasted about twelve. Nothing material passed at Northleach, Mrs. Lee wished not to set out for Gloucester till it was dark, however the post-chaise was ordered, and they set out about four o'clock for Cheltenham, where having changed horses they arrived at the Bell Inn at Gloucester, about seven o'clock on Tuesday evening. Mrs. Lee ordered dinner; Loudoun examined the bed chamber and bed linen, as on the two preceding nights. Mrs. Lee went to bed about ten o'clock, and Loudoun soon followed her. On Wednesday morning Mrs. Lee got up in an exceeding good humour, she had slept the preceding night in one of Loudoun's shirts, whilst her own chemise was washing.

She promised Loudoun that she would rise early in Wales and take exercise on horseback before breakfast: their mode of life in Wales was settled. She said to Loudoun, "in short I ex-pect to be quite *en bon point* before I have been there many weeks," he replied, "it shall not be my fault if you are not," she laughed at the idea. Mrs. Lee frequently during the journey, asked Loudoun if he thought Lockhart would, as he had promised, join them on Wednesday at Gloucester and bring her cloaths with him. Loudoun constantly replied that "she might rely on it, that Lockhart held his promises and engagements too sacred not to keep them." Mrs. Lee appeared to expect Lockhart with much anxiety, and she frequently asked during Wednesday, at what hour the mail arrived at Gloucester. Mrs. Lee and Loudoun had a long conversation after breakfast, she entered into a detail of her circumstances. she said that that she had a mortgage upon an estate in Ireland, the interest of which was badly paid, that she was confident from the knowledge which she had of Lockhart that he would readily have justice done her, and that she meant to communicate the particulars of that mortgage to Lockhart. She took a full review of her fortune, after which Loudoun said, " this is the first time Mrs. Lee that you have thought proper to enter so minutely into your pecuniary affairs, and I therefore wish you to understand that it is sufficient for me to know them, but I have resolved to have no concern whatever in the management of your fortune." Mrs. Lee observed that Loudoun "must of course manage both herself and every thing relative to her." Loudoun said, " if you think I can do justice to you by pointing out what may relieve your cares, I am willing to undertake the management of your person, but as to your fortune that must remain under your own controul."

About two o'clock Loudoun went out of the room in which Mrs Lee was sitting, he returned in about ten minutes, and saw Mrs. Lee in the passage looking wild and frantic. The waiter of the Inn, and Miller the Bow Street Officer were with her. Davidson the female servant pointed out Loudoun to the officer, Miller immediately came up to Loudoun and said "I have a warrant against you Mr. Gordon, I am told you have pistols," Loudoun replied "you need not be frightened, my pistols are locked up and the case is in my chamber; if you have any thing to say to me pray follow me." Loudoun then took Mrs Lee by the hand, and led her into the room, Loudoun read the warrant, and as soon as Mrs Lee had read it, she took Loudoun's hand, and kissing it, said to Miller, the Bow Street Officer, "you must not take him away, (meaning Loudoun,) poor fellow, like a common felon, he has done nothing, it is too bad to send a warrant after him, it is a base and most unwarrantable liberty." Loudoun seeing the frantic state of Mrs Lee's mind, sent Davidson who was in the room, to procure some lavender drops, which Loudoun administered to her, and endeavoured as much as possible to quiet her fears with regard to himself. As soon as Mrs. Lee was a little restored, the mail coach, which stops at the Bell Inn, where Loudoun and Mrs. Lee were at Gloucester, passed the window, Mrs Lee arose, opened the window and looked eagerly to see whether Lockhart, for whose arrival she had constantly expressed an anxious wish, was arrived in it, and not seeing Lockhart come out of the mail, she spoke of her disappointment to Loudoun; which Miller, who had been all the time in the room, hearing, said "that he believed the person we were looking for was not come." Mrs Lee asked Miller how he knew whom we were looking for?" He answered "I suppose you expect Mr Lockhart," Mrs. Lee said "yes, where is he?" Miller replied that "Lockhart was in confinement." Mrs Lee appeared astonished and grieved at the intelligence. She asked Miller "what he intended to do with Loudoun." Miller answered "Mr. Parkin gave me orders to bring Loudoun and yourself to London as soon as possible" As that was the case, Mrs Lee expressed a wish to have dinner before her departure from Gloucester, which was ordered. Mrs Lee went into her bed chamber to dress herself, and Loudoun sent for his pistol case, which he gave into the charge of the Bow Street Officer. Loudoun recollecting that he had some bank notes in the pistol case, unlocked it before Miller, took them out, and was about to take some other papers which were in the pistol case, when Miller took them and said " I have orders to take all papers from you," " I understood at Tetsworth that you wanted Mrs. Lee to sign some paper Loudoun replied " yes I did want Mrs. Lee to sign a letter to her servants, at Tetsworth, for Lockhart to take with him to London, that Mrs Lee's servants might not refuse to let Lockhart have her cloaths, which she wished him to obtain for her, that is the only paper I ever asked Mrs. Lee to sign; the papers you found in the pistol case, you may read and put them into the fire if you choose, they contain nothing but the expences upon the road and the route." Miller replied " he should burn nothing." Mrs. Lee came into the room and requested Miller to go outside the door that Loudoun and herself might converse privately for five minutes, this request Mrs. Lee repeated and was complied with two or three times at Gloucester. Mrs Lee then said to Loudoun " I am sorry to find from Davidson that they (meaning her servants) have taken the harshest measures in their power, but however keep up your spirits " Mrs Lee made some other remarks and saluted Loudoun several times, when Miller came into the room. They all three sat down to dinner together, and Mrs. Lee particularly requested Loudoun to eat heartily, which she said would give her much pleasure. A post coach and four was ordered that they might set out after dinner. Mrs. Lee after having drank two glasses of rum and water, which Loudoun mixed at her request, said she was ready. During the dinner at Gloucester, Mrs. Lee said to Miller "is it not shameful to send a warrant to apprehend him, meaning Loudoun, I am sure nobody can look in his face and say that he is a rascal, and they certainly have acted to him as if he was one, by sending a Bow Street Officer after him" Miller replied "I never heard any one say he was a rascal nor does he look like one." Just before dinner Miller wrote a letter, and Mrs. Lee said to him, when he was going to seal it, "you must let me see it," Miller then gave it to Mrs Lee and she told Loudoun afterwards it was a letter to Mr Parkin, saying *that* he had taken Loudoun into custody and that he should be in London to morrow, Thursday, with Loudoun and Mrs. Lee. Mrs Lee, Loudoun, Miller, and Davidson, set out in a post coach and four between four and five o'clock, from the Bell Inn, in which, after changing horses at Northleach they went to Witney, where Mrs. Lee was desirous of supper, they supped, the post coach could go no further. Mrs. Lee finding that we should be obliged to go on to Oxford in two post chaises, earnestly requested Miller to permit Loudoun and herself to go in one, whilst Davidson and Miller went in the other. Miller would not consent to it, but offered to let them go in the same post-chaise together, provided he was also with them. Loudoun thinking that would render Mrs Lee uncomfortable, advised her to go with Davidson, and that Miller and himself would go in the other post-chaise. Mrs. Lee appeared to like the ale at Witney, Loudoun ordered two bottles of it to be put into the post-chaise for her. She made Loudoun eat heartily at supper Before they left Witney, Mrs. Lee again begged Miller to let her converse privately with Loudoun, she said that "she wished as they were to be divided, that Loudoun wherever they stopped to change horses during the night would come into her post chaise." He did so at Oxford and at Tetsworth. They arrived at Tetsworth about five in the morning, and Miller told Mr. Edmonds "that Mrs Lee loved Loudoun like her own dear eyes."

They arrived at High Wycombe between eight and nine on Thursday morning, when Loudoun handed Mrs. Lee out of the post-chaise, they were shewn into a room, Mrs. Lee said to Miller "I don't know what they mean by making us travel all night in such haste to London, it is a most extraordinary circumstance and uncommon affair altogether, and Mr. Miller I am now unwell and shall not be able to leave Wycombe for three or four hours, as I wish to rest myself a little." Nothing particular passed, Mrs. Lee made Loudoun eat an additional quantity of eggs. After breakfast Loudoun saw an account of the elopement in the Sun of Wednesday the 18th of January, that Lockhart was committed for further examination, which he shewed to Mrs. Lee, she was quite dispirited, and having first saluted Loudoun, said, "come keep up your spirits, you know it all depends upon me, and you may rely upon it I shall never hurt you" At Wycombe also Mrs Lee requested Miller to leave Loudoun and herself together for a few minutes.

There being no post-coach to be had at Wycombe, Mrs. Lee again asked Miller to permit Loudoun and herself to go in the same chaise without him. Miller would not. They set out about twelve o'clock from Wycombe, and dined at Uxbridge, before dinner Mrs Lee again requested Miller to go out of the room and leave her alone with Loudoun, which when the Bow Street Officer had complied with, Mrs. Lee said to Loudoun "I am very sick Loudoun, and have been so both yesterday and the day before, and I am convinced that it is the sickness of conception, if you choose Loudoun, I am willing to pass the remainder of my life in your society, and should you be taken to prison, you may rely upon it that I will share with you your confinement." Loudoun said " he could agree to any thing which she wished but that of allowing her to share his confinement with him, to which he never could assent." Mrs. Lee then said "I promise if you wish it, to pass the remainder of my life with you." Loudoun assented, Mrs. Lee then saluted him and gave him a promise of eternal fidelity. Mrs. Lee told him to appear dejected on the journey. She, after dinner, said to Miller, "what are you going to do with this young man when we arrive in London?" Miller replied that "Mr. Parkin had ordered him to conduct Loudoun and Mrs Lee to Mr. Parkin's house before they went any where else." Mrs. Lee on hearing it, begged Miller to leave Loudoun and her alone together, he did, she said to Loudoun "that she should wish to see Lockhart or a legal friend that lived in the Temple, before she went to Mr Parkin". Loudoun told Mrs. Lee "he was well convinced that Mr. Parkin would persuade her to act as he chose in this business," and added that "Mr. Parkin was an interested man." Mrs Lee replied that "Mr. Parkin had never been able to make her do as he chose hitherto, I am sure that he will not in this instance." Mrs. Lee allowed the truth of Loudoun's observation that Mr. Parkin was interested for his own character. When Miller returned into the room, she requested that he would take her to Lockhart before she went to Mr. Parkin, Miller said he could not, she repeated this request two or three times before they arrived in London, Miller would not grant it. Mrs Lee finding he would not let her see Lockhart, requested she might go to a friend in the Temple before she went to Mr. Parkin, that Miller also refused repeatedly

They arrived in London about seven o'clock and drove to Mr Parkin's house, Mrs. Lee and Davidson got out there, and after waiting about an hour, Mr Parkin told Miller that he " might take Mr. Gordon into confinement and bring him to Bow Street about eleven o'clock to morrow." Mr Parkin said " that he had seen Mr. Bond that morning, upon the receipt of Miller's letter, and it was agreed that the examination should be on Friday." Miller told Loudoun in the way to the watch house, that the first question Mr. Parkin asked him was, " whether he had kept Loudoun separate from Mrs Lee during the journey," and which it appeared Mr. Parkin ordered Miller to do.

On Monday the 23d, Mr. Blackett called upon Loudoun in the New Prison, Clerkenwell, and said that " Mrs. Lee desired Mr Blackett to tell Loudoun that she intended to keep the promise which she had made to him "

Loudoun received a message from Mrs. Lee

on the 1st of February, 1804, in the following words. "I am very sorry that I cannot send you any money, which Mr Parkin has prevented by stopping fifty pounds for the expedition of the Bow Street Officer to Gloucester "

Loudoun a few days after this message, received another from Mrs Lee, in the following words. "I hope you will form no connection during your confinement with the sex." Loudoun returned no answer to either of these messages from Mrs. Lee.

On Monday the 17th of January, Mr Parkin, who acted in the double capacity of Attorney and Trustee for Mrs. Lee, applied to the sitting Magistrate (Mr Robinson) in Bow Street, for a warrant to apprehend Lockhart and Loudoun Gordon, which was granted. Mr Lockhart Gordon was apprehended about eleven o'clock that night, by Miller and Atkins, two of the Officers belonging to the Public Office. Mr Lockhart Gordon was confined in St Martin's Watch-house during the whole of Monday night, and was conveyed in a hackney coach to Mr Parkin's house in Great Ormond Street, by the Bow Street Officers, on Tuesday Morning the 17th of January. Miller, one of the officers, had represented Mr Parkin to be a "perfect gentleman."

Mr. Lockhart Gordon told Mr. Parkin that he was ready to confess his guilt in having carried away Mrs. Lee, provided Mr. Parkin would give him his word and honour that Loudoun should not be prosecuted. Mr. Parkin would not give that promise, which Lockhart in vain endeavoured to extort, by declaring himself guilty of a crime he had not committed, in order to save his brother from the horrors of imprisonment. Lockhart informed Mr. Parkin that Mrs. Lee and Loudoun would be at Gloucester on Wednesday, and desired him to send her cloaths immediately. Mr. Parkin having obtained all the information he wanted, told the Officer to "take him away," Mr. Lockhart Gordon was conveyed to the Public Office in Bow Street and placed at the bar.

EXAMINATION

MR BOND AND SIR WILLIAM PARSONS,

Two of His Majesty's Justices of the Peace

FOR THE

COUNTY OF MIDDLESEX

———

MR BOND said, " I know nothing of these parties " The warrant was then shewn to Mr Bond,
and Janet Davidson, one of Mrs Lee's servants, was
called and said, " that the prisoner at the bar had
dined with her mistress, at her house in Bolton Row,
on Sunday last, that soon after dinner Mrs Lee rang
the bell in her bedchamber, which Davidson answered, and found Mrs Lee crying, and very much
agitated Mrs Lee said to Davidson, ' there is a plan
to take me out of my house ' Davidson replied, ' who
dare take you out of your own house ' Mrs Lee answered, ' they have pistols, and I am afraid they will
force me out of my house ' Mrs Lee also told Davidson ' *to watch, but not to say any thing.*' Mrs. Lee
returned into the drawing-room in a few minutes
afterwards Mrs. Lee's footman was sent by Davidson

H

to call a hackney coach, whilst he was gone Davidson heard her mistress say 'I will not be taken out of my house,' which induced her to go with her fellow-servant to the assistance of her mistress, when she saw the Mr Gordons endeavouring to force her mistress down stairs, who was resisting them Davidson attempted to rescue her, upon which Mr. Lockhart Gordon took a pistol from his pocket, which he put to Davidson's head, and swore he would shoot her if she made the least noise or resistance Davidson was much alarmed and ran into her mistress's bedchamber with an intention to open the window and call for assistance, but she was so much terrified that she could not find the window, hearing the street-door shut she came down stairs and went into the street, when she saw the post-chaise driving off, upon which she cried out 'Fire! murder! thieves' they have stolen my mistress' She also saw the prisoner last night about eleven o'clock, when he came to her mistress's house in a hackney-coach He got out of the hackney-coach and said, 'Well,' and came into the passage of the house seeing a stranger there, he said, 'Are you a peace officer?' to which Davidson did not hear any answer given. Mr. Lockhart Gordon returned into the hackney-coach, and ordered the coachman to shut the door; he looked out of the window of the hackney-coach, and said to Davidson, 'Come here, I want to speak with you' He had a pistol in his hand, she said, 'I will not come whilst you have that pistol in your hand.' Mr. Gordon then ordered the coachman to drive away he had not gone many yards when the coach stopped, and Mr Lockhart Gordon jumped

out, she saw him soon after in custody of the Bow
Street officers.

Janet Davidson then swore to the truth of her deposition.

Sarah Hunt, servant to Mrs Lee, was called, and
said, " that the prisoner at the bar had dined at her
mistress's house on Sunday last with his brother.
Some time after dinner she heard Mrs Lee say, ' I
will not be taken out of my house' She went up
stairs with her fellow-servant Davidson to her mistress's assistance, Mr Lockhart Gordon presented a
pistol to her breast, and swore that he would shoot
her if she made any noise or resistance. Mr. Lockhart Gordon said to his brother, " bring her down, or
I will shoot you ' Loudoun forced Mrs Lee down
stairs, and out of the street door. Mr. Lockhart
Gordon held Sarah Hunt, and swore that ' he would
shoot her if she did not go up stairs·' She being much
alarmed went up stairs to her fellow-servant Davidson,
and afterwards went into the street, where she saw a
post-chaise driving very fast away, which she believed
her mistress was in." She confirmed Mr Lockhart
Gordon's having been at her mistress's house last
night, as sworn by Davidson

Sarah Hunt swore to the truth of her depositions.

William Martin, servant to Mrs Lee, called. He
said, " that the prisoner and his brother had dined
with his mistress on Sunday last Soon after dinner
the dining-room bell rang violently he answered the

bell, when Mrs Lee went out of the dining-room, and ran up stairs. some time after he was sent by Davidson, his fellow-servant, for a hackney-coach: As he was coming back he heard his fellow-servants crying out, 'they have stole my mistress,' and seeing a post-chaise drive off very fast, he followed it, and endeavoured to overtake it in vain. He went to Mr Robert Lee's house with his fellow-servants, and not finding him at home, he went to Mr Parkin, and told him what had happened. He saw the prisoner again on Monday night, when he came to his mistress's house in a hackney coach, he got out, came into the passage, and said, 'Well,' seeing a stranger in the passage. Mr Lockhart Gordon asked whether he was a peace officer. Martin did not hear whether any answer was made. He felt something in Mr Gordon's left-hand pocket, which he thought was a pistol, and went out to procure assistance, and met two watchmen not far from his mistress's house, he was coming back again he saw Mr Gordon going away in a hackney coach. the servants were calling 'He's gone! He's gone!' Martin told the coachman, 'that if he did not stop he would knock him off his box' one of the watchmen stopped the coach, when the prisoner jumped out with a pistol in each hand, and swore he would shoot the first rascal that attempted to stop him. he ran away towards Clarges Street when he was taken into custody in a few minutes by the Bow Street officers.'

William Martin swore to the truth of the above statement

Miller, the Bow Street officer, was called. He

said, " he went with Atkins to Mr Lockhart Gordon's lodgings on Monday evening, about ten o'clock, and found that Mr Lockhart Gordon had dressed himself there that evening and was gone to a ball in Portland Place, they followed him to Portland Place, and found that he had been there but was gone, they were going to Mrs Lee's house in Bolton Row to see that all was safe there, when they heard the watch-mens rattles, and on coming to the spot where a great crowd was assembled, they were informed that it was Mr Lockhart Gordon who had a pistol in each hand, one of which Miller took from him, which he pro-duced, and which proved to be loaded, the other was taken from him by one of the watchmen '

Miller swore to the truth of his deposition

John Sharman and another watchman were called, who said, " they had just gone their rounds when William Martin came and desired them to assist him in securing a man who had ran away with his mistress, they followed him, and William Martin perceiving a hackney-coach driving along, told them to stop it, which they did by striking one of the horses on the head, a gentleman then jumped out of the hackney-coach, and ran down Clarges Street, where they took him into custody, on the Bow Street officers coming up they delivered the prisoner into their charge."

Both the watchmen swore to the truth of the above deposition

Mr Blackett was called, and said, " he had known

the prisoner and his brother seventeen or eighteen years, that he had taken Deacon's Orders about three months, and that Mr Loudoun Gordon was an officer in the army ' Mr Lockhart Gordon thanked Mr Blackett as he was going out of Court, for the gentlemanlike and proper evidence which he had given

Mr Parkin then read the Statutes of the 3d Hen. VII. c 2 and 39 Eliz c 9 and appealed to the magistrates, whether they did not think the evidence which they had heard read was sufficient to warrant a commitment of the prisoner under those statutes. After some consultation between Mr Parkin and the magistrates, it was agreed that the prisoner should be committed to Tothill-Fields Bridewell for further examination upon Tuesday the 24th Mr Bond then said to the prisoner, " then on Tuesday, Mr Gordon." The prisoner answered, " very well, Mr Bond "

On Friday, the 20th of January, Mr. Lockhart Gordon was most unexpectedly informed by Atkins, the Bow Street officer, that he was ordered to take him to Bow Street immediately When Mr. Lockhart Gordon was placed at the Bar, he told Mr. Bond that he was very much surprised at Mr Bond's conduct, in having brought him to the Bar on that day, Friday, the 20th of January, when Mr Bond himself had declared that Tuesday, the 24th of January, would be the day of his re-examination He thought Mr. Bond's conduct particularly improper, as it was his intention to have had the assistance of counsel Mr Bond said, " that the reason for which he had been brought up on that day was, that had his offence been only a misdemeanour he might have been admitted to bail" Mr Gordon said, "that when a man gave him a promise, he always expected him to keep it, and told Mr Bond that he did not believe a word he said" Mr Loudoun Gordon was then also brought to the Bar, when Mrs Lee's deposition, which had been taken in private, was read as follows

She said "she had been acquainted with the Gordons about thirteen or fourteen years, that about two months ago their acquaintance with her was renewed, by Loudoun Gordon calling on her in Bolton Row, at which time nothing particular passed, but since this she saw Loudoun Gordon three times, and in company with Mr Lockhart Gordon, previous to Sunday last That she having had a dream, she communicated the same to Mr Loudoun Gordon, he shortly afterwards replied to it by letter, therein stating an interpretation of the dream She received two other letters afterwards from Mr. Loudoun Gordon, testifying the great regard and esteem he had for her, and the last of the two letters stating that his brother, Lockhart Gordon, would protect her at the risk of his life and fortune. In the course of the week previous to Sunday last, Mr Loudoun Gordon called upon her, when she invited him to dinner on Sunday last, as well as his brother, whom she had once seen with him before and accordingly, a few minutes before five o'clock, they came. Nothing particular passed during dinner, nor until Lockhart Gordon took out his watch, and observed to his brother, "it is near seven o'clock, the chaise will be here at seven," upon which Mrs Lee asked what chaise? when Lockhart Gordon replied

(addressing himself to Mrs Lee), "you go with
Loudoun to-night,' and that, either before these
words were spoken, or after, Lockhart Gordon said
to his brother, "you have got a present for Mrs Lee,"
to which Mrs Lee replied, "I am determined not to
take any present," when Mr Lockhart Gordon desired his brother to come and fetch it, who came, and
Lockhart Gordon produced a plain gold ring, desiring
his brother to put it on Mrs Lee's finger, which
Loudoun Gordon attempted to do, but she refused to
let him, and the ring was laid upon the table Shortly
after, Mrs Lee arose, and attempted to go out of the
parlour, when Lockhart Gordon went to the door, and
told her she should not go out, she told him she
wished to go up stairs, but Lockhart Gordon persisted
she should not go out of the room, and shewed a
pistol, at which time she thought Lockhart Gordon
desired his brother to go and see if the chaise was
ready —She then opened her parlour door, and went
up stairs into her bed-room, where she met Davidson,
her female servant, to whom she said, "I am afraid
there is a plan to take me out of my house to-night,'
who replied, "who can take you out of your own
house " in answer to which Mrs Lee observed, "they
are armed with pistols, don't say any more, but
watch' Mrs Lee then returned down stairs into her
drawing-room, where Loudoun Gordon came to her,
and requested her to go down stairs, observing the
chaise was ready In a few minutes after, Lockhart
Gordon came into the drawing-room, and said to his
brother " don't stand there " when Lockhart Gordon
took hold of one of Mrs Lee's arms, and pulled her
to the door, saying, "you shall go I am deter-

mind,' to which she replied, " I am determined
not to go out of my house, what right have you to
force me out of my own house" To which Lockhart
Gordon replied, " I am desperate," at which instant
she observed Davidson, her female servant, coming
towards her, followed by her other female servant,
when Davidson came up, and endeavoured to rescue
her mistress from Lockhart Gordon, a scuffle then
ensued between Lockhart Gordon and the servant,
and they went down stairs, leaving Loudoun Gordon
with Mrs Lee, Lockhart Gordon then called to
Loudoun Gordon, and said, " bring her down, or I
will shoot you " At this time her mind was in such a
distracted state, she had no recollection whether
Loudoun Gordon forced her down stairs or not, and
continued in that state until she found herself in a
post-chaise into which she had been hurried by Lockhart and Loudoun Gordon, both of whom she found
in the chaise when she came to herself, and the first
thing she recollected was, hearing Lockhart Gordon
calling out to the post-boy to drive on with speed, or
he would shoot him They changed horses at Uxbridge and Wycombe, but could not tell whether they
had any refreshments, she did not get out of the
chaise till they got to Tetsworth, where they arrived
at midnight, the family at the inn were gone to bed,
and they were called up to get them supper, which
was ordered by Lockhart Gordon, she partook of the
supper at this time she was perfectly in her senses,
and observed to Lockhart Gordon, it was a breach of
hospitality to take her from her own house without her
consent, and that she thought it one of the most infernal measures that ever was taken she entreated to

have a chaise to take her back to London, to which
Lockhart Gordon answered it was impossible to be
complied with, Mrs Lee then said she saw it was
inevitable, and went to bed under an impression that
her life was in danger from Lockhart Gordon, and
permitted Loudoun Gordon to come to bed to her.
On Monday morning they all breakfasted together,
when Lockhart Gordon observed, that she would have
no cause to repent the measures that had been taken,
for that it would be the object of his brother's life to
render her happy, and that as to himself, he would
adhere to her as long as he had blood in his veins, and
he would be one of the best friends she ever had.
After breakfast Lockhart Gordon set off for London,
and she, at the earnest entreaty of Loudoun Gordon,
went forward with him to Gloucester."

Mr Lockhart Gordon put two very material questions to Davidson, the female servant. The first was,
how long she supposed it was between the time Mrs.
Lee came out and said to her the M. Gordons were
armed with pistols, and was afraid they would take
her away, and the time they brought Mrs Lee out of
the drawing-room, and took her into the chaise, to
which she answered, about twenty minutes.

The second question was, if the man-servant was in
the house at the time her mistress said they were
armed with pistols, and was afraid they would take her
away? which she answered in the affirmative.

When that part of Mrs Lee's evidence was read, in
which she stated her having said to Davidson, " they

are armed with pistols," Mr. Lockhart Gordon said, with peculiar emphasis and energy of expression, " You know in your own soul, Mrs Lee, that Loudoun had no pistols, remember there is another world, and although you do not believe it, there are many here who do, and who will be shocked to hear you swear to such an infamous falshood For my own part, I had determined to stand my trial in silence, had you not prosecuted my brother, of whom you know that you were once doatingly fond, but I am now resolved not to spare you an inch " Mrs Lee replied, " I have been tenderly alive to both your situations, and as far as I have been able have endeavoured to save you, remember that it is not the first time that your lives have been in my power "

In consequence of the unfounded conjectures which were formed by the public, owing to Mrs Lee's having made use of so artful an insinuation, Mr Lockhart and Mr Loudoun Gordon thought it necessary to request their Solicitor would obtain an explanation, which they might be enabled to publish in their justification

The following letter was written by Mr Hanson to Mrs. Lee.

6th February, 1801.

MADAM,

As various unjust conjectures have been formed, in consequence of an expression which the public prints have represented you to have made, at Bow Street, on Friday, the 20th of January, concerning Messrs Gordons, viz. "this is not the first time your lives have been in my power."

Mr. Gordon and his brother being convinced that it is not your wish to conceal the truth in this instance, they hope that you will do them the justice to state, that you could not possibly allude to any thing that took place previously to the 15th of January last. Requesting to be favoured with your answer,

I have the honor to be,

MADAM,

Your humble servant,

J. HANSON.

Mrs. Lee

=====

Mrs. Lee's reply to Mr. Hanson

Sir,

The phrase I made use of on the day of the examination in Bow Street was, " I have been tenderly alive to your situations, recollect I *had* your lives in my power," alluding to their having been at my disposal at Tetsworth, when, had I alarmed the neighbourhood, they would have been taken in the act of my assistance, and *must* have incurred the severest penalty of the law.

I am, Sir,

Your obedient humble servant,

J. A. LEE

Bolton Row, Feb. 8, 1804.

Mrs Lee told Mr Hanson's clerk, to whom she gave the above letter, that she did not allude to any thing which took place previously to the 15th instant, January

Mrs Lee's letter is a striking proof of her extreme ingenuity, and is couched in such ambiguous terms, as Mrs Lee was well aware would tend rather to criminate than to exculpate the Gordons.

On Friday, the 27th of January, Mr Lockhart and Mr Loudoun Gordon were brought from the different prisons in which they were confined, to Bow Street, and had a conference with Mr Serjeant Best (who kindly attended as their friend, at the express desire of the Earl of Portsmouth, to whose unbounded generosity they are inexpressibly indebted) and Mr Abbot their Counsel, they were placed at the bar of the Public Office Mr Lockhart Gordon addressed himself to Mr Bond, the senior magistrate, and said, ' I regret, Sir, that my ignorance of the forms of justice should have induced me to make use of some expressions which have been thought improper, I own, Sir, that I felt myself much hurt at being unexpectedly brought a second time to this bar, which prevented my having the assistance of Counsel, and that appearance of countenance and support from my family and friends, which every gentleman in my unfortunate situation must naturally wish to have. I trust that you, Sir, and Sir William Parsons will think what I now say a sufficient apology.' Mrs Lee made the following addition to her former evidence, when the prisoners were fully committed for trial

" On the Monday morning, after breakfast, while they were at Tetsworth, in a conversation with Lockhart Gordon, in consequence of which, whether well or ill founded she could not tell, he appearing at that time in a distracted state of mind, and not knowing what he said, she delivered a note, addressed to her female servant Davidson, at her house in Bolton Row, Piccadilly, beginning with " No money, no cloaths, death or compliance,' which she requested Mrs Edmonds, the landlady of the house, to forward as directed.'

The informations of all the witnesses were read previous to Mrs Lee leaving the office, and a few additions were made to their former accounts, but which were not worth noticing

Mr Parkin's deposition was read, stating that "he had known the said Mrs Lee, late Rachel Fanny Antonini Dashwood spinster, for upwards of seventeen years, and who about the year 1794 intermarried with Matthew Allen Lee, Esq that soon after the marriage a settlement was made of Mrs Lee's property by the Court of Chancery, by which a moiety of her property was vested in the trust of Mr Parkin and three other gentlemen, who were authorised to pay a certain sum to Mrs Lee for her own sole and separate use, that in the year 1795 a separation took place, when it was agreed that Mrs Lee should receive 1000l per annum for her life, and which had been paid to her ever since that period, she continuing to live separate from her said husband, who was still living.'

Mr Bond asked Mr Lockhart Gordon if he had any thing to say, to which he replied, not a word, he left his case to his Counsel

Mr. Bond then put the same question to Mr. Loudoun Gordon, who gave a similar answer to his brother.

Mr Abbot then addressed the magistrates, and said, the prisoners having left the management of their defence to him, he should defer what he had to offer on that head until the day of trial, when he had no doubt they would be able to justify their conduct

The parties were then bound over to prosecute at the next assizes for Oxfordshire, the offence having been committed in that county

Mr Lockhart Gordon said to Mr Bond, " As this is the last time that we shall probably meet, I hope, Sir, that no bitterness remains in your mind on account of what has passed."

Mr. Bond replied, " Mr Gordon, your present conduct does you infinite credit, and I assure you that no bad impression of what has passed will remain upon my mind, and I do most sincerely wish you a favourable issue of your trial "

TRIAL, &c.

OXFORD ASSIZES,

Monday, March 5th, 1804;

Before Mr. Justice Lawrence & Mr. Justice Le Blanc.

LIST OF THE GRAND JURY.

The MARQUIS OF BLANDFORD, FOREMAN.

Rt Hon. Francis Lord Spencer	Charles Browne, Esq.
Sir Christopher Willoughby	Charles Brown Mostyn, Esq.
John Fane, Esq.	Thomas Toovey, Esq
Oldfield Bowles, Esq	William Henry Ashurst, Esq.
William Lowndes Stone, Esq.	Robert Peers, Esq.
Thomas Stonor, Esq.	George Clarke, Esq.
Francis Penystone, Esq.	John Bush, Esq.
John Spencer, Esq	Francis Wastie, Esq.
Henry Calveley Cotton, Esq	William Fermor, Esq.
George Frederick Stratton, Esq	Michael Corgan, Esq.
John Lenthall, Esq.	William Jemmett, Esq
Alexander James, Esq	

Mr. JUSTICE LAWRENCE then addressed the GRAND JURY in the following SPEECH, which he took from Notes

GENTLEMEN,

"IT will not be necessary for me to detain you long, explaining the law on the different cases now to be brought under your consideration. They are but few in number; the most considerable I am able to speak more fully of to you, from my having seen the Examinations at Bow Street, and that which will require your most attentive consideration, is the one founded on the Act of the 3d of King HENRY VII which makes it a capital Felony for any person forcibly to take away a woman for the purpose of enjoying her property, marrying her, or defiling her person. This Statute very properly provides for the safety of those, who, either by hereditary descent, marriage, or any other means, come into possession of considerable property, who would otherwise be liable to fall a prey to violence and injustice Now, in order to prove a felony, and bring it within the meaning of the Statute, it is necessary that I should state to you that three things are requisite, in order to prove the crime, against which this Statute was wisely enacted, and has since been particularly enforced In the first place, the Statute supposes that the woman is possessed of property secondly, that the person who takes her away is actuated with the lucre of gain, and has a design upon that property, and thirdly, that he takes her off, either with the design of marrying her, or violating her person —With regard to the first, it is supposed that a woman has property, but when she is married, she cannot have any property of her own, however, if her affairs are in the hands of trustees, and her property invested with them, it amounts to the same thing, and is equally felony, and comes within the meaning of the Statute Secondly, it is supposed that the possession of property lays at the foundation of this crime, and that the person offending is instigated by the hopes of obtaining it, which he endeavours to accomplish by illicit means, and to prevent which this Act was very properly made, for if the property of women, whether hereditary or howsoever entailed on them, be not secured by law, infinite mischiefs would accrue to society, by the rapacity and profligacy of individuals The third thing necessary to constitute the crime, is the marrying the woman, forcibly taking away or defiling her person, it is hardly necessary that I should explain to you what this means, it signifies that carnal knowledge or connection between the sexes, which, when force is used, would be denominated a rape. In order to constitute this a capital offence, it must be proved that force has been used. and, in order to bring it within this indictment, it must be shewn that force has been used in this county Now, though force may have been used in another county, if it is not proved to your satisfaction, that it has been continued in this county, where the indictment is laid, you cannot receive such evidence as sufficient to warrant the conviction of the prisoners, but if the evidence adduced before you be sufficient to prove that force has been continued in this county, that will be sufficient to establish the guilt of the prisoners, who will then become liable to the penalties of the Statute. Suppose a man who is indicted for larceny, steals goods in one county and exposes them for sale in another, he is guilty of stealing them in the place where he carries them, and is obnoxious to punishment equally as if he had stolen them there.—Gentlemen, if the fact of force be proved to your satisfaction, that is, if she has been forcibly brought out of another county into this, against her own inclination, and by compulsion from the prisoners, it will be sufficient to criminate them, and it will not be material to enquire, whether the defilement of her person took place by force, or with her own consent. This distinction would have been necessary in the case of a rape, but the charge here is of a more serious nature, and depends entirely upon the question, whether force has been used to bring her into this county. Gentlemen, you will decide on this case, in proportion to the evidence you receive, and make your report accordingly.

The Grand Jury, after sitting several hours, and examining sixteen witnesses, returned at six o'clock, *A true Bill against Lockhart and Loudoun Gordon.*

TUESDAY, MARCH 6th, 1804.

AT seven o'clock Mr Justice Lawrence entered the Court, attended by the Sheriff, &c. when the prisoners were brought in, and delivered at the Bar.

LOCKHART GORDON, aged 28 years.
LOUDOUN GORDON, aged 23 years

Brought March the 2nd, by Habeas Corpus, from London, charged on the oaths of Rachael Fanny Antonina Lee, wife of Matthew Allen Lee, Esq and others, with feloniously and unlawfully taking the said Rachael Fanny Antonina Lee from her house in Bolton Row Piccadilly, against her will, for the lucre of substance, and defiling her at Tetsworth, in the County of Oxford contrary to the Statute, &c.

The Clerk of the Arraigns proceeded to call over the names of those gentlemen who had been summoned by the Sheriff to attend as Jurymen The Court was occupied for the space of near two hours, before a Jury was impannelled the prisoners and prosecutor challenged a considerable number A Jury was, however, at length compleated and sworn, consisting of twelve Englishmen, the prisoners from their appearance, had the utmost reliance that their verdict would be given according to their conscience

A list of the Jurors was applied for the day before, but could not be procured by the prisoners' Counsel, which accounts for the number of their challenges.

LIST OF THE PETTY JURY

W Bullock, FOREMAN	John Willis
William Jones	Thomas Faulkner
Robert Heritage	William Brooks
Thomas Lucket	Thomas Giles
Richard Higham	Samuel Huckfield
Daniel Walford	James Parker

FOR THE PROSECUTION,

COUNSELLORS—Milles, Dauncey, and Puller

Anthony Parkin, Esq SOLICITOR.

FOR THE DEFENDANTS,

COUNSELLORS—Abbot and Peake.

John Hanson, Esq SOLICITOR

Mr Pugh, Deputy Clerk of the Assize, read the Indictment, which consisted of several counts, which charged them, generally, with forcibly taking, seizing, and carrying away Rachael Fanny Antonina Lee, for lucre of substance, from her house in Bolton Row; and after defiling her at Tetsworth, in the County of Oxford, to the great displeasure of Almighty God, to the disparagement of the said Rachael, to the discomfiture of her friends, to the evil example of others, against the form of the Statute, against the king's peace, his crown, and dignity —To this Indictment the prisoners pleaded *Not Guilty,* and were immediately put upon their deliverance Mr Puller opened the pleadings, when Counsellor Mills opened the case.

He said, " it was a most painful duty which was imposed upon him to address the Jury in a case like the present, a case altogether new, and almost unprecedented; accompanied by the most outrageous intentions, and in which the offending parties were men possessing, in an eminent degree, the polish of gentility, and the refined advantages of high birth and elegant education, these rendered the crime which they had committed still more flagitious and unpardonable than if they had been in a lower situation, in which they might have been supposed not to have known better. Neither of them are mature in years, they should therefore have been looking forward with laudable emulation to the attainment of reputation, it is an aggravated crime in these men, who are placed above necessity, to have been instigated by the unworthy motives, for which the law provides a proper punishment, and which it is my duty to lay down. Before he stated the case, he begged the Jury to give particular attention to one thing, namely, that they would not be biassed by the false and scandalous reports which had been spread by wicked and ill-intentioned persons against the lady who was the Plaintiff on the present occasion, reports which were infamous in their nature, and should be consigned to a deserved oblivion. He did not mean to say that the prisoners had spread these reports. He told them, that a British Jury, the purity of which was the corner-stone of our constitution, was called upon to judge with unbiassed and unprejudiced minds, and to attend only to the evidence which was delivered before them in a court of justice, expelling from their minds all partiality, and forgetting whatever they may have heard in other places. This was a case, he said, entirely new to them, but the act of parliament on which the present prosecution depended was so exact, that when they had heard and considered the evidence which he should bring before them, they could have no difficulty in giving a fair and impartial judgment upon it He then read extracts from the Act (3 Hen. VII) which, though made nearly four hundred years ago, defined, he said, exactly the present case—It was an act made for the protection of women, in their three different stages of maid, wife, or widow, and it enacted, that any person who, for lucre of gain, forcibly carried away and married any maid or widow, or defiled a wife in the absence of her husband, was subject to the penalty inflicted for felony After this act had been passed one hundred years, the benefit of clergy was taken away from it, and the punishment was, in consequence, since that time, a capital one Many had suffered who came within the reach of this act, and he thought he should prove that the prisoners were in that situation The question was, whether they had taken away a woman by force out of her own house, having goods in her possession and whether she was defiled by Loudoun Gordon He begged their particular attention, then, to three points, 1st. to the time and manner of the prosecutrix being seized and carried off. 2d to the events that happened between that time and their arrival at Tetsworth, in Oxfordshire, and 3d to the act of defilement which took place there.

But, Gentlemen, I must forewarn you, that before you can find them guilty of this crime, you must be satisfied that force has been used in this county, now though force may have been used in another county, unless it is proved to your satisfaction that the force was continued into this county, you cannot find the prisoners guilty

He trusted, that when he traced the progress of the acquaintance of the prosecutrix with the prisoners, and their subsequent conduct, they would judge with facility the intent of the offence committed, and whether any defence which could be opposed would be sufficient to justify the crime of which they were accused

"Mrs Lee he then stated to be the natural daughter of the late Lord Le Despencer, who died in 1781. He left two illegitimate children, Mrs Lee, and a son She was born in Dec 1773 At his death, Lord Le Despencer left 40,000l to Mrs Lee; and he should prove that she was in the receipt of 1200l a-year at the time when this unfortunate affair happened, of which one half was at her own disposal, in case of her death without issue At her father's death, having no relations, and her mother not being a woman proper to have the charge and education of her daughter, being a woman of very bad character, she remained till the age of fourteen under the care of guardians At that time she was put to school under Mrs Gordon, mother of the prisoners, where they of course resided. The eldest of the Gordons was of the same age with Mrs Lee, the second six or seven years younger Their acquaintance thus began in the days of innocence She staid there a year From the year 1790 to 1803 she had never seen or heard of either of the prisoners During that time Mr Lee paid his addresses to her, being a ward in chancery, and under age, she could not give her consent, they therefore eloped to Scotland, and were married according to the rites of the Scottish church at Haddington, March 9, 1794. On his return, Mr Lee was confined in the Fleet for some time for this offence. A settlement was made on Mrs Lee, dated Feb 9, 1795, by which she had 500l a-year pin-money at her own disposal. Their tempers not agreeing, they were separated Jan. 4, 1796, since which time she had no one to protect her, as she only lived a short time with her brother, who afterwards went abroad. Her establishment was one man and two maids, her income 1200l a-year, and she lived sometimes at Bath, and sometimes in other places. Being of a retired disposition, and very seldom going out, she gave herself very much up to books, which in the end rendered her very nervous, and injured her health. In Nov 1803, she first heard of Loudoun Gordon from Mr. Blackett, an apothecary, who had long attended her. He had enquired after her she remembering him, said, " she should be glad to see him," in consequence of which he called upon her, and she received him in an hospitable manner as an old acquaintance. Loudoun soon found out her weak part, and immediately began to work upon it, at one of the interviews which he had with her, of which he only had five in all. He proposed a scheme for their travelling together into Wales; she rallied him upon it, but finding he pressed the subject, turned it off by relating a dream which she had had. He here observed, that the dream which had been inserted in the different public papers was as different from the original one as any two things possibly could be her's being one of the most chaste and innocent nature. The interpretation Mr Mills said was admirably written, and doubtless did great honour to the composer of it During all this time she had not seen Lockhart, but hearing he was in town, she testified a desire to see him.

On the 12th an extraordinary correspondence took place; Loudoun called upon Mrs Lee and left three letters, two from himself and one from his brother. (After having read Loudoun's letter, Mr Milles said, " what trash, what rhapsody ') During this time Mrs. Lee had no conception that the defendants had any idea of pressing either the journey into Wales or any other expedition. Mr. Mills then proceeded to give some account of the Gordons Lockhart had lived two years at Mrs. Westgarth's, Alsop's Buildings, New Road, London, Loudoun was but just returned from the West Indies The latter expected to be arrested on the 14th of January, he gave particular caution to Mrs Westgarth not to admit any one to him till after twelve at night, when it would be Sunday. Previous to this, he had been arrested for ten pounds, which had been discharged by Lord Portsmouth's Solicitor At this moment Mr Milles said, there are three detainers for debt lodged at the gaol against Loudoun Gordon He then described what took place, as afterwards related by Mrs Westgarth, Mrs. Lee, and her servants, relative to her being carried off, and took occasion to insist on the shameful behaviour of Lockhart in this instance, who was a clergyman; for Loudoun, he said, was struck with the heinousness of the crime he was going to commit, and was heard by Mr. Edmonds, the landlord of the Inn at Tetsworth, arguing upon it with his brother, who told him that if he did not go to bed to Mrs Lee he would shoot him. This was also an additional proof that Loudoun was not influenced by love for Mrs Lee, for if he had been, would he have hesitated a moment when she was in his power, and when he might enjoy her without the least fear of interruption or hindrance? Instead of which, he could not be compelled to do it but by the most violent threats. The next morning they breakfasted at eleven o'clock, at two Lockhart went away.—Why did he not go before?—The reason was plain, he would not leave his brother till the thing was done. He went from thence to London on Monday, when he went to a ball in the evening. At eleven at night he went again to Mrs. Lee's house, where, on knocking, and the door being opened, he saw a strange face, he immediately asked, "Are you a peace officer?" He insisted on this as a strong proof of a guilty conscience, which interpreted every unknown person as an officer of justice. Being afterwards taken, and desiring to speak to Mr Parkin, Mrs. Lee's Solicitor, he told him he was the only person to blame, as he had forced his brother into it, and would certainly have shot him if he had not acted as he did, he therefore desired his brother's name might be struck out of the warrant. Mr Parkin of course refused to do this. Lockhart wrote the word Gloucester on a piece of paper, by which an arrangement was made for Mrs Lee's recovery and for Loudoun's apprehension. While at Tetsworth, Mrs Lee, after explaining her situation to Mrs Edmonds, the landlady, gave her a letter, which she begged might be put into the post after she was gone, as she was, during the whole time, in the greatest agitation. The letter was addressed to her maid Davidson, as follows: " Davidson,—No money, no cloaths!—Death or compliance."—This was her last act. From all which circumstances he concluded she was carried away by force, for the lucre of substance, and that the force was continued in the county of Oxford.

Mr Mills described Mrs. Lee as seated in the chaise between terror and provocation, and concluded a vapid and uninteresting speech of two hours and a half, by expressing the greatest confidence that such a shameful and infamous action would meet with the punishment it so richly deserved, and that a proper exercise of justice in this case would be an awful warning to every one, that female innocence would always find the strongest protection in the laws of our country "

Sarah Westgarth lives at No 8, Alsop's Bildings— Lockhart Gordon had lodged three years at her house, was sometimes backward in his payments, had joined with Loudoun in security for ten pounds, for which they had both been arrested This was immediately discharged by a clerk of Lord Portsmouth's Solicitor. Lockhart owes her twenty-six pounds for lodgings, besides sixty-four pounds, for which he gave her a note not yet become due. Loudoun ordered her on Saturday, the 14th of January, not to admit any one to him, as he was afraid of being arrested Told her to order a chaise and pair to Uxbridge, to be at the corner of Bolton Row, Piccadilly, at seven o'clock in the evening, and to put in it a portmanteau, box, and pair of boots of Lockhart's, she did so accordingly, and went with it to the place, she remained in the chaise till Loudoun came, and told her she might go home. Lockhart returned to her house on Monday, dressed in the evening for a ball, and went out. (Cross-examined by Mr. Abbot) Does not know any thing of the Mr. Gordons family, Lord Portsmouth often comes to them, does not know what ball Lockhart was going to; is in the habit of giving him credit for his lodgings

Janet Davidson lives at No 4, Bolton Row—Has lived fifteen months as lady's maid with Mrs. Lee, had lived twelve years in Mr Lee's family; never saw the Gordons till they went to Mrs. Lee's house, saw Loudoun first in December, 1803. He only came four or five times, the first time he called he saw Mrs Lee; the second time he came in the evening; that time Davidson was sent to fetch Mr. Dashwood's picture, (Mrs Lee's brother) for Mr. Loudoun Gordon to look at; the third time he came at eleven o'clock at night, he did not see her mistress that night, Mrs Lee was gone to bed, the family were up, the next time he called she gave him a letter from Mrs. Lee, after reading it Loudoun tossed up his head, and asked if Mrs. Lee would be at home in the evening, was answered " No," he however called and was let in. On the 15th he and his brother, who had only called once before, dined there, they came about five; very few minutes after their arrival went to dinner, the dinner was carried back into the kitchen about six, the servants dined upon it, she went up stairs after her dinner; Mrs Lee ordered tea and coffee before dinner, after dinner she heard the parlour bell ring violently, she ran up and found her mistress standing in great agitation in the drawing-room, in the dark, she appeared in great distress, was crying and rubbing her hands, and said, " They have a plan to carry me away " Witness said, " Who can dare carry you out of your own house." Mrs Lee said, " They have pistols " Witness argued with her upon it, to convince her it was impossible she should be taken by force from her house Mrs Lee said, " Don't say any thing; watch, but don't leave the house." Saw afterwards Loudoun, who told her to send the man for a coach, sent him accordingly As soon as he was gone, heard a scuffle, and her mistress say, " I am determined I will not be forced out of my own house" Lockhart said, " I am desperate " Witness ran up stairs with the cook, the drawing room door was open, found him holding her round the waist, and forcing her down stairs, Loudoun was standing close to him; witness put her arms round her mistress to keep her back, and said, " You shall not take her out of her house ' Lockhart took out a pistol, and said, " Woman, let her go, or I will shoot you." The pistol was presented to her head, she said, " Are you a Gentleman." He said, " It is no matter what I am." She said, " I am going down stairs." He said, " If you go down stairs I will shoot you " Loudoun said, before she quitted Mrs. Lee, " Woman, she shall go " The footman was absent all this time. She let her go, and Lockhart laid hold of her gown, she at last got away, and ran up stairs in the dark, intending to open the window and alarm the street, but was so frightened she could not; heard the street door shut, and the other maid calling out, " She's gone! She's gone!" Ran out into the street, the post chaise door was not shut, she saw nothing but the door i-jar, she exclaimed, " Murder! Fire! Thieves! They have stol n my mistress " The post-chaise set out The footman returned with a coach, which he left, and ran after the chaise, but could not overtake it During the whole time no consent on her part appeared She did not alter her dress, which was a muslin gown, with small crape on her head, her mistress was a very nervous woman, reads and writes a great deal, had been very uneasy all the morning of Sunday, saw no preparations whatever for any journey Saw Lockhart again on Monday night at eleven o'clock, he knocked at the door, and when he saw the footman and another man in the passage, took out a pistol, and said, " Are you a peace officer?" Did not hear the answer Lockhart then ran out to his hackney coach, and called from the window, " it was the witness he wanted to speak to." Witness said, " she would not speak to him while he had a pistol in his hand" Footman and watchmen then came up, he jumped out and ran away. Saw him brought back afterwards by Bow-street officers. Received the letter which her mistress sent from Tetsworth on Tuesday. (Cross-examined by Mr Abbot) Loudoun had only been admitted three or four times; he was with her mistress for an hour and an half by himself one evening Mr Loudoun Gordon staid once a considerable time, no third person being present, she was not acquainted with Mrs Lee's habits of life before she entered into her service, Mrs Lee went into her bed-chamber on Sunday evening, and came down voluntarily into the drawing-room Her mistress wore a steel necklace with a bag of camphor hanging to it, had worn it some time. When Lockhart called he left his card, as her mistress was not at home. She is melancholy, and has been so some time. Had not gone to church since Witness lived with her. (Examined again) When she saw her mistress in the drawing-room, her eyes rolled very much, seemed very much affected, had never seen her so much affected before.

Sarah Hunt—Said, she had lived with Mrs Lee fifteen months as maid of all work, Mrs Lee lived very retired, knew only a few people, her society was small. Three weeks since she first saw Loudoun, only saw him once before Sunday the 15th Saw Janet Davidson when she came down from the drawing room, on the evening of the 15th of January, who told her that her mistress was in a great fright, that she had ordered her to stay in the house and watch what was going on. They accordingly went to watch in the back parlour, after listening a quarter of an hour, heard a noise, and the Gordons talking very loud, heard Mrs Lee say to Lockhart Gordon, " You are determined on my ruin." He answered, " I am desperate " There was then a scuffle on the stairs, and she heard her mistress say, " she would not be forced out of her own house " She then went up stairs, and found her on the stairs, and the two Gordons pulling her down. Heard Lockhart say to Davidson, " Woman she shall go " Davidson then wanted to run down stairs, Lockhart said, " Woman, if you do, I will shoot you " Witness had then hold of one of her mistress's hands, to prevent her from being carried away. Lockhart said, " If you make any noise, and do not let go your mistress, I will shoot you " She then let go her hand, saw Lockhart's pistols presented, and heard him say to his brother, " Take her out, or I will shoot you " Lockhart held her, while Loudoun forced out her mistress Lockhart then let her go, went out, and shut the street door after him, she immediately ran up stairs to Davidson, calling out that her mistress was gone; they then ran out into the street, but the chaise was gone, and she only heard the noise of the wheels, the hackney-coach then came which the footman had been for, he ran after the chaise, but not being able to overtake it, returned, got into the hackney-coach, and went in it to Bow Street. Heard a double knock at the door on Monday night, at eleven o'clock, when it was opened, saw Lockhart Gordon and a hackney-coach in the street, he on entering the passage, said, ' Well!" and then seeing a man in the passage with the footman, asked him whether he was a peace officer, and directly went out again to the coach, after getting in he looked out of the window, and said to Davidson, " It is you I want to speak with " She answered, " I will not speak with you while you have that in your hand " Witness did not see that he had any thing in his

K

hand Said her mistress was very fond of books; never went out, and knew very few people (Cross-examined) When she first came into Mrs. Lee's service, she lived at Woodford, during the whole time of her service, her mistress had been but twice to church, once at Woodford, with Lady Wright, and once at Minehead, in travelling. Knew that a man of the name of William Roberts once lived with her as footman, was sure that in pulling her down stairs Loudoun had his arm round her waist.

William Martin, sworn—Said that he was footman to Mrs Lee. On Sunday, January 15th, at five o'clock, the Gordons came to dine with his mistress, after dinner he took away, and went into the kitchen, about an hour after he heard a noise in the parlour overhead, as if the chairs were moved about, and people were running round the table the bell was then rung violently, ran up stairs, but could not get into the parlour, because somebody held the handle of the lock in the inside, the door at length opened and his mistress ran up stairs, to all appearance very much flurried. Went into the parlour, and saw Lockhart Gordon put something into the inside pocket of his coat. asked if any thing was wanted, on being answered, No, returned down stairs, the maid then came down, and said her mistress wanted a light in the drawing-room, took one up, thought she looked very much frightened, met Loudoun on the stairs, going up; Lockhart went up after him, heard his mistress say, " Lockhart Gordon, you are determined on my ruin " Did not hear Lockhart answer; the drawing-room door then shut, and soon after the maid told him to go for a hackney-coach he accordingly went for one, and returning with it, heard the maid calling out, " Murder! They have stolen my mistress!" Left the coach, and ran after a chaise, which he saw driving off, as far as Park Lane, and then lost sight of it, he then returned, and went to Bow Street in the hackney-coach, to give information of his mistress being carried off. The night after heard a knock at the door at eleven o'clock, went up stairs with a man whom he had procured to sit with him, saw Lockhart at the door with an opera hat on, Lockhart said, " Well!" Witness got behind him, and felt something like a pistol in the inside of his coat, Lockhart then said to the man, " Are you a peace-officer?" Witness immediately went for a watchman, and returning with him, heard the women crying out, " Murder!" &c. and saw a hackney-coach driving off, he ran up and seized the reins of the horses, and told the coachman that he would knock him off his box if he did not stop   The watchman a^t length succeeded in stopping the coach, Lockhart then jumped out with a pistol in each hand, and said, " I will shoot you " While he stooped to avoid the pistol, Lockhart ran away   They pursued him, and overtook him in Clarges Street, he had a pistol in each hand, and said he would shoot the first rascal that offered to seize him   They however took him, and afterwards delivered him to Miller the Bow street officer, who happened to meet them. (Cross-examined)   Once when Loudoun called, he said his mistress was not at home, when she heard his voice she asked him up   Has called in all about eight or nine times, staid generally alone with her, and remained a considerable time, two hours or more, has heard the name of John and William Roberts mentioned, but does not know where John Roberts now lives, has heard Mrs. Lee had a footman of the name of Roberts, Loudoun one evening brought three letters for Mrs Lee, took one letter from his mistress to Loudoun on the 1st of January, he called one evening and brought three letters, he delivered them to Mrs Lee, Loudoun staid in the parlour, and was afterwards shewed into the drawing-room, Mrs. Lee seldom eats supper, and it did not wait for Mrs. Lee that evening, he staid about two hours, might stay till ten, he never refused Mrs Lee to Loudoun, who called seven, eight, or nine times upon his mistress.

George Hunt, sworn—Said he was a postboy, in High Street, Mary-le-bone, Mrs Westgarth ordered a chaise to be brought to Allsop's Buildings, he drove one there, and took her to the end of Bolton Place, at about seven o'clock, she told him to wait till the gentlemen came, and also waited there herself In half an hour one of the gentlemen came, and called to him to move across the street immediately, and wait there, Mrs Westgarth went home, in a quarter of an hour afterwards a gentleman and lady came towards him, the chaise door was open, he thought the lady was laughing, they came up to the chaise, she got in, and he after her, another gentleman then came, got in, and shut the door, ordered him to drive to Uxbridge as fast as possible, and told him to drive on as fast as he could or he would shoot him. Witness paid turnpikes, did not observe that the lady made any resistance, he drove to Uxbridge in an hour and an half, received half-a-guinea for himself from one of the gentlemen, who went into the house while the chaise was changing, did not hear any screaming when he set off from Bolton-street, did not assist in changing the luggage at Uxbridge, the Uxbridge chaise drew up alongside of the other, did not see the company go from one chaise into the other (Cross examined) The lady came walking along the street, with the gentleman, the lady was laughing, he saw the gentleman hand the lady into the post chaise, he was looking that way, another gentleman came a few minutes afterwards, the lady appeared to come very willingly; there was nothing that induced him to suppose that the lady was carried off by force There were four men about the post chaise at one time at Uxbridge, the lady did not ask for assistance; Lockhart was in the inn at that time. She might have had assistance at Uxbridge, the waiter was ordered to take some porter to the post-chaise, of which the lady partook. He said the gentleman gave him half-a-guinea, it was very good pay, and what the gentleman chose to give him. He said that gentlemen often said to him, " Drive on or I will shoot you."

Thomas Gamby sworn—Said he was a post-boy at Uxbridge, did not see how the company got from one chaise to the other, drove them to Wycombe, heard one of the gentlemen ask the lady whether she would stop at Wycombe, or go on to Tetsworth, she answered she did not care, one of the gentlemen got out and paid him, they staid at Wycombe about 20 minutes.

Joseph Powell sworn—Said he was a post-boy at Wycombe, drove two gentlemen and a lady to Tetsworth, where they got out, carried the luggage into the room where they were, took in two pistols and some other things, one gentleman and the lady were standing by the fire, they went through the kitchen that she might not wet her feet (Cross examined.) While at Tetsworth, the Worcester coach and the Mail were in the yard, he saw two passengers of the Worcester coach standing in the yard of the inn (Examined again.) One of the gentlemen found fault with him for not driving faster, he answered, he must have drove him in two hours at farthest, or he would not have beat the Mail.

Rachel Fanny Antonina Lee sworn—Said she was married to Mr Lee, at Haddington, in Scotland, in 1794, and was not re-married in England, was not then of age, Mr Lee was confined in the Fleet by the Chancellor, for having ran away with her, they were separated in a year and an half, and have lived separate ever since, since that time has been in the receipt of 1200l per annum, separate income, entirely at her own disposal, was 7 years old when her father Lord Le Despencer died, went at 14 years of age to Mrs Gordon's, at Kensington, her situation, in point of fortune, was known there, she staid there almost a year, Lockhart and Loudoun Gordon were there in the holydays, she saw them often, but had never seen either of them since 1790, or been at all acquainted with their circumstances till December 1803, at that time she heard Loudoun was in town from her apothecary, Mr Blackett, and that he had enquired after her, she understood he was just returned from the West Indies, and wished to send her some present· she said "she should be happy to see him," Loudoun accordingly called, he staid with her between 1 our and two the first visit, the subject of their conversation was, the death of his sister, he came again some ' y after, and in all he called four times by himself, and once with his brother, he staid sometimes two hours with her; she always read and wrote a great deal, their conversation often turned upon books, on the second interview Mrs Lee warned Loudoun against any particular attachment to her, she thought it likely as he was young, he replied, that " his happiness was in her hands," to turn the conversation, she related to him a dream, after this she read him two interpretations of the dream, which were both political, he requested to take it home, he did so, he sent an interpretation to it, she has destroyed it, she saw him twice after the dream, once when he called she ran down stairs and told him she could not see him then, having somebody with her, remembers sending him a note, in which she said that she supposed his intoxication was the cause of his calling so late, at the third interview, he proposed to her to take a tour with him into Wales, she talked about it, reasoned against it, and at last refused it, never agreed to any time of going off with him, never heard of any preparations for the journey, nor ever consented to it, received two letters on the 12th of January, the proposition mentioned in the one from Loudoun, related to the journey into Wales (The letter was here produced, and she identified it.) She had told him to absent himself from her for some days previously to her receiving Loudoun's letter of 12th January The following letter was read

January 12, 1804

MY DEAREST MADAM,

If you assent to my proposition, I shall gain an inexhaustible source of felicity, you will lose the pity of the ignorant and the prejudiced   The protection that I have to offer to you, Madam, is the strength of body and mind, the courage and the life of a man, not unused to danger My age, Madam, has been matured by adversity, the only school of true philosophy, my situation, though it is not what I could wish, nor what my education and birth might have led me to expect, is rendered less irksome, by the possession and enjoyment of that inestimable treasure, mens conscia recti, which can neither be purchased nor stolen. I have consulted my heart, and would have plucked it out had it dared to think you less than the most perfect of human beings   I have consulted my reason in a low, but clear voice, it whispered praise   Pleasure, name it not my heart, for I have found no traces of you imprinted there. If the union of congenial souls can be rendered more complete by the union of their bodies, obey Madam the first mandate of God and of nature, or tremble at the thoughts of your disobedience   The world, Madam, is unworthy of you, the false opinion which it will probably form with regard to your conduct, will never be able to shake your constancy or fortitude   In obedience to your commands I have communicated your letter to my brother, he respects, he

admires you, and he says that he will protect you at the
hazard of his life and fortunes   I can feel, though I cannot
express what I am to you, more than that I am,

   My dearest Madam,

    Your sincere and affectionate

      L. H GORDON.

Mrs Lee said that Loudoun's letter was in answer to one
which she had written to him, she only remembered one
sentence of her own letter

Lockhart s letter was then produced, but not identified,
the man-servant brought them up, she received them both
at the same time, does not recollect seeing Loudoun Gordon on Friday, nor that the footman brought up any letter
but a note in answer to the invitation to dinner she had sent
them.   The *following letter was then read*

       January 12, 1804.

MY DEAR MADAM,

   I consent with all my heart to every thought,
word, and expression contained in Loudoun's answer to
your letter, which you did me the honour to desire him to
communicate to me   If Loudoun deceives you Mrs Lee,
I will certainly blow his brains out, and then we shall both
be eternally damned as we shall most richly deserve Strong
feelings burst the fetters of ceremony, and express themselves in the untutored language of nature.   Mrs Lee will
find in Lockhart Gordon a friend who has a head to conceive, a heart to feel, and a hand to execute whatever may
conduce to Mrs Lee's happiness

   I have the honour to be, &c.

      L. GORDON.

Does not remember that Loudoun called on her on the evening of January the 12th. During Loudoun's visit on the 12th, she invited him and his brother to dinner on Sunday the 15th, begged Loudoun that Lockhart and himself would come to her as friends, the invitation was after she had received the two letters, she said she would talk about Loudoun's plan with Lockhart and himself on Sunday, did not see either of them between the 12th and 15th of January, nor had any communication with them, on the 15th they came to dine with her, before dinner she said to Lockhart, " What do you think of this extraordinary plan your brother has proposed?" Lockhart answered, " If you love Loudoun, and Loudoun loves you, it will conduce to the happiness of both." She said, " have you reflected upon the consequences of the measure?" he answered, " Mrs Lee, you will gain two friends, have you a friend that would shed his blood for you" she said, " No, I have friends to lose,' nothing about leaving London was then said. They went down to dinner, and the conversation turned on various subjects. Nothing led her to suspect, nor had she ever any idea that any journey was intended. After dinner Lockhart said to Loudoun, " you have a present for Mrs. Lee," Lockhart said, " Come and fetch it," Loudoun went to him, and took the ring, which he tried to put on her finger, but which she resisted, and it was laid on the table, soon after Lockhart said, " It is near seven o'clock, and the chaise will be here at seven," she said, " What chaise?" Lockhart answered, " You must go with Loudoun to-night" she treated it as a joke, and joked upon it, does not know how long it was before she went up stairs, when she did, Lockhart opposed her, he then produced a pistol, she was panic struck; did not ring the bell in the parlour, did not see her man-servant when he came into the dining-room, after Lockhart had shewed the pistol, Lockhart told Loudoun to go and see if the chaise was ready, he went, she went up stairs to her room, saw her maid Davidson, and told her there was a plan to take her out of her house, Davidson said, " How can they take you out of your own house ·" she said, " they have pistols " She then went down stairs to the drawing-room, Loudoun came in and was alone with her in the drawing-room, Loudoun asked her to go, and said the post chaise was ready, she said she could not go, Lockhart soon came up, and said, " Do not stand there, I am determined you shall go, ' taking her at the same time by the arm, she said, " she would not go out of the house," he said, " I am desperate " Mrs Lee recollects Davidson coming up and attempting to part Lockhart from her, a scuffle ensued, she cannot speak as to the pointing of the pistol, was not absolutely stupified, she does not remember the other servant coming up with Davidson, heard Lock-hart say, " Bring her down, or I will shoot you, ' he was then on the middle of the stairs, and she at the top, she went down with Loudoun, when she got into the passage, saw Lockhart pointing at the other maid with a pistol, they then got her out into the street, where she saw a chaise; had no idea beforehand of the chaise being prepared, does not remember in what relative situations she was in, in her way to the chaise, with regard to Lockhart or Loudoun, and cannot say how she got in, having such a vague idea about it, remembers perfectly saying in the chaise, that she was in a state of stupefaction, she spoke principally to Lock-hart, to induce him to let her return, she begged to have a chaise to return, Lockhart said, it was impossible, did not get out of the chaise, except when she got from one chaise to the other remembers that Lockhart said something about the ring, and that Loudoun put it on her finger, she remem-bers being left in the room at Tetsworth with Lockhart, re-monstrated with him, and said, she thought it was one of the most infernal measures that ever was taken, and a breach of hospitality to take her out of her own house she again

begged to have a chaise, which he refused; the maid asked
when she should be in bed, and when she should light the
gentleman up, she said in about ten minutes; she was ap-
prehensive that a serious scuffle might ensue, in which lives
might be lost, if she did not comply, whatever might have
passed in the chaise implying assent, and notwithstanding she
was in her senses when they sat down to supper, had she
had the perfect exercise of her mind, she should have been
more inclined to have ordered a post chaise than to have gone
to bed; had her affection for Loudoun been ever so violent,
under such circumstances she would not have wished to have
indulged it, she was quite a stranger in Tetsworth, and knew
nobody to apply to, Loudoun staid all night with her, and
she did not deny that she submitted to his embraces, they
got up at half-past eleven, the maid came to their room in
the morning, and took her gown to be washed, as she had
no change of cloaths, went down to breakfast, and saw
Lockhart, her mind was confused, she does not recollect
Lockhart's going away from Tetsworth, saw Mrs Edmonds,
the landlady of the inn, after Lockhart had gone away;
there was no acquaintance between them, communicated
her situation to her, and entrusted her with a letter for her
maid Davidson, in the chaise remembers hearing Lockhart
say, he wished to be in town the next evening to a ball.

Mrs Lee, did that intercourse which usually takes place
between man and wife, take place between Loudoun and
you at Tetsworth?

It did

(Cross examined by Mr Abbot) Knew that the late
Lord Portsmouth was Mrs Gordon's brother, Mr. Gordon
was dead, he was brother to Lord Aboyne, Lockhart and
Loudoun used to come home for the holidays, when an acquaintance commenced between them.

The ring was put on her finger during the journey to Tetsworth, by Loudoun, she does not recollect that Loudoun mistook the hand, nor rallying him for having done so, she cannot say that it did not pass. The ring first occurred to her about a fortnight or three weeks ago, her servant, Davidson, told her that she (Mrs Lee) had just taken off a strange ring, she could not recollect saying 'in compliance with the custom of the world I consent to wear this ring," she could not say it did not pass, she recollected that Lockhart wished to return to Town, to go to a ball, that he might not be suspected to be concerned in the elopement, she thought it a very villainous thing, because it would make it appear that she had gone away with Loudoun, that appeared to be his motive. She did not hear what family he was to meet at the ball, did not consent to his returning to London. Mrs Lee knew before Sunday night that Lockhart was about some arrangement relative to a living, he said it would be to his interest to return to town, that he might appear at the ball and consolidate his interest, he said " that she ought to consider his prospects would be destroyed if she did not consent to his return to town," she replied " that he had destroyed her prospects" She considered Lockhart as the person who had led to the whole of the affair, he alone made use of any violent expression, he alone had expressed the determination that she should leave her house, Loudoun was as much subservient to Lockhart as she herself. Mrs Lee said that she had her steel necklace on when she left her house on Sunday night, that she threw it out of the post-chaise window; she could not say whether it was before she arrived at Uxbridge or not, she said "that was her charm against pleasure," when she threw it out of the window, at that moment she gave herself up, she afterwards expostulated, a bag of camphor hung to the necklace, the word charm alluded to one of the supposed properties of that medicine, she used it as a sedative, it is supposed to calm the passions, particularly that passion which subsists between one sex and the other. She did not recollect desiring the post-chaise might be drawn up close to the other at Uxbridge, she could not say it was not so, she recollected Lockhart leaving the post-chaise at Uxbridge, but did not recollect that she drank porter there. She recollected Lockhart talking something about his health; some enquiries were made about Loudoun's health, the enquiries were made by herself. Mrs Lee was satisfied that Loudoun's health was unimpaired, this was in the course of the journey to Tetsworth, Mrs. Lee might, she said, have enquired in the post-chaise on Sunday night, how long it had been since Loudoun had connected himself with a woman, she recollected that Lockhart said Loudoun had not been out at night. Mrs Lee sent advice to both brothers during their confinement in Newgate, to abstain from a connection with the sex which might be most prejudicial to them. That advice was not sent to Loudoun in particular. Mrs Lee might have desired in the post-chaise that the sheets should be well aired at Tetsworth. Mrs. Lee said she eat a good supper at Tetsworth, that the conversation was about Hieroglyphicks and Grecian Architecture, from the whole of the conversation her conduct certainly was such as to induce Loudoun to suppose he might come to bed to her. She first heard Loudoun's return from the West Indies of Mr Blackett, who, Mrs Lee said was a very respectable apothecary, and had attended her for thirteen or fourteen years, she told Mr. Blackett to tell Loudoun that she should be very glad to see him. His first visit was upon the 14th of December, Mrs Lee recollected that Loudoun saluted her that day, and that he was in the habit of saluting her when he called, but Mrs Lee said that no further familiarities passed between them, remembered appointing a day for Loudoun to come to her again, on his first visit, she recollected receiving a letter from him for not coming upon the day she had fixed upon. Remembered desiring Loudoun to tell his brother that he need not be afraid to call upon her, although he was a clergyman, because her religious opinions were sceptical, she never denied that her opinions were sceptical, she had not attended places of divine worship for some years, Mrs Lee said that the doctrines which are preached there did not accord with her's, and added, that she did not believe in christianity.

As soon as Mrs Lee had said that "she did not believe in christianity," Mr Abbot, whose abilities during Mrs Lee's cross examination and that of other unwilling witnesses, had been very conspicuous, discontinued his questions.

A conference between the judge and the counsel on the part of the prosecution then took place for some minutes, afterwards the counsel on both sides conferred together, and Mrs. Lee was given to understand by them, that there was no farther occasion for her evidence. Mr Justice Lawrence desired Mr Anthony Parkin to protect Mrs Lee out of court, after some hesitation Mr Parkin exhibited himself upon the council table, which he had to cross in order to overtake Mrs Lee. Mr. Edmonds, master of the Inn at Tetsworth, was called to the the bar, in order probably to cover Mrs Lee's retreat.

Mr Justice Lawrence said to the jury "it did not appear that any force had been used to bring Mrs Lee into the county of Oxford, and observed to them that Mrs Lee might have had assistance at the different turnpikes through which she passed on the road to Tetsworth, as well as at the inns where the horses were changed, you must therefore acquit the prisoners." The jury immediately pronounced the prisoners "not guilty."

Mr Justice Lawrence addressing himself to the prisoners said "their acquittal was no cause of triumph to them, as their conduct had been disgraceful "

Mr Abbot exacted a promise from Lockhart, just before the Judge made his observations upon their conduct that he would not speak, which promise was the cause of his silence.

A gentleman behind the bar wished Lockhart joy, he said "I thank you Sir, and am only sorry that I have not had an opportunity of clearing my character from the aspersions which have been thrown upon it." Some noblemen and several gentlemen kindly and voluntarily appeared in court to give their evidence in favour of the prisoners.

Lightning Source UK Ltd.
Milton Keynes UK
UKOW02f1340090314

227800UK00011B/567/P